grandma's best

100 everyday recipes

First published in 2013
LOVE FOOD is an imprint of Parragon Books Ltd

Parragon Inc.
440 Park Avenue South, 13th Floor
New York, NY 10016

Copyright © Parragon Books Ltd 2013

LOVE FOOD and the accompanying heart device is a registered trademark of Parragon Books Ltd in Australia, the UK, USA, India, and the EU.

www.parragon.com/lovefood

ISBN: 978-1-4723-1376-8

Printed in China.

Notes for the Reader

This book uses standard kitchen measuring spoons and cups. All spoon and cup measurements are level unless otherwise indicated. Unless otherwise stated, milk is assumed to be whole, eggs are large, individual vegetables are medium, and pepper is freshly ground black pepper. Unless otherwise stated, all root vegetables should be washed in plain water and peeled prior to using.

For best results, use a food thermometer when cooking meat and poultry. Check the latest USDA government guidelines for current advice.

Garnishes, decorations, and serving suggestions are all optional and not necessarily included in the recipe ingredients or method.

The times given are only an approximate guide. Preparation times differ according to the techniques used by different people and the cooking times may also vary from those given. Optional ingredients, variations, or serving suggestions have not been included in the time calculations.

Recipes using raw or very lightly cooked eggs should be avoided by infants, the elderly, pregnant women, convalescents, and anyone with a weakened immune system. Pregnant and breast-feeding women are advised to avoid eating peanuts and peanut products. People with nut allergies should be aware that some of the prepared ingredients used in the recipes in this book may contain nuts. Always check the packaging before use.

grandma's best

introduction

The kitchen is the heart of the home and, for many, Grandma is the heart of the kitchen. It was G
who created wonderful culinary memories for us, and we yearn for those delicious foods that evok
memories of home cooking. You'll find all those recipes—and those memories—in this collection.

There's a range of simple but satisfying dishes from warming soups to quick pasta dishes tha
instant comfort. Try Mushroom Bruschetta or Corned Beef Hash for a leisurely brunch. Or Fried
Wings or Steak Sandwiches for a quick snack after a busy day.

All the recipes you need to create the perfect weekend lunch are here, from roasts and
satisfying stews and casseroles. To accompany these are the essential side dishes—perfect roast p
homemade gravy, and delicious vegetables. These are sure to impress family and friends and w
warm memories for the next generation.

dessert, you are spoiled with choices with a whole chapter of delicious dishes—from winter

like Bread and Butter Pudding and Pumpkin Pie to summer treats such as Banana Splits.

irresistible smell of warm baking is the essence of Grandma's home cooking, and this section

whole range from simple cookies and muffins to special celebration cakes. There's also a couple

htforward bread recipes that will fill the house with tempting aromas. These may just disappear

ey have had time to cool!

ether you consider yourself an experienced cook or are just starting out, we're sure that this

n will soon become a well-used treasure. In *Grandma's Best—100 Everyday Recipes*, you'll find a

nd delicious range of recipes, and each one comes with clear step-by-step instructions and photos

ntee results just as good as Grandma's!

simple but
satisfying

tomato soup

ingredients

serves 4

4 tablespoons butter
1 onion, finely chopped
3¾ cups tomatoes,
    finely chopped
2½ cups hot chicken stock
    or vegetable stock
pinch of sugar
2 tablespoons shredded fresh basil
    leaves, plus extra sprigs,
    to garnish
1 tablespoon chopped fresh
    parsley
salt and pepper
chili oil, for drizzling (optional)

method

1 Melt half the butter in a large, heavy-bottom sauce
   Add the onion and cook over a low heat, stirring
   occasionally, for 5 minutes or until softened. Add t
   tomatoes, season to taste with salt and pepper, an
   cook for 5 more minutes.

2 Pour in the hot stock, bring back to a boil, then re
   the heat and cook for 10 minutes.

3 Push the soup through a sieve with the back of a
   wooden spoon to remove the tomato skins and s
   Return to the saucepan and stir in the sugar, rema
   butter, basil, and parsley. Heat through briefly, but
   not allow to boil.

4 Ladle into warmed soup bowls. Serve immediatel
   garnished with a sprig of basil and a drizzle of chi
   if using.

split pea & ham soup

ingredients

serves 6–8

2½ cups green split peas
1 tablespoon olive oil
1 large onion, finely chopped
1 large carrot, finely chopped
1 celery stalk, finely chopped
4 cups chicken stock or vegetable
    stock
4 cups water
1½ cups lean smoked ham,
    finely diced
¼ teaspoon dried thyme
¼ teaspoon dried marjoram
1 bay leaf
salt and pepper

method

1 Rinse the peas under cold running water. Put them i
saucepan and cover generously with water. Bring to
boil, and boil for 3 minutes, skimming off the foam f
the surface. Drain the peas.

2 Heat the oil in a large saucepan over a medium hea
Add the onion and cook for 3–4 minutes, stirring
occasionally, until just softened. Add the carrot and
celery and continue cooking for 2 minutes.

3 Add the peas, pour over the stock and water and st
to combine.

4 Bring just to a boil and stir the ham into the soup. A
the thyme, marjoram, and bay leaf. Reduce the hea
cover, and cook gently for 1–1½ hours, until the
ingredients are very soft. Remove the bay leaf.

5 Taste and adjust the seasoning. Ladle into warmed
soup bowls and serve.

chicken noodle soup

ingredients

serves 4–6

2 skinless chicken breasts
4 cups water or chicken stock
3 carrots, sliced into ¼-inch slices
3 ounces egg noodles
salt and pepper
fresh tarragon leaves, to garnish

method

1 Place the chicken breasts in a large saucepan over a medium heat, add the water and bring to a simmer. Cook for 25–30 minutes. Skim any foam from the surface, if necessary. Remove the chicken from the stock and keep warm.

2 Continue to simmer the stock, add the carrots and noodles, and cook for 4–5 minutes.

3 Thinly slice or shred the chicken breasts and place in warmed serving bowls.

4 Season the soup to taste with salt and pepper, and pour over the chicken. Serve immediately, garnished with the tarragon.

steak sandwiches

ingredients

makes 4 sandwiches

8 thick slices white or
   whole-wheat bread
butter, for spreading
2 handfuls mixed salad leaves
3 tablespoons olive oil
2 onions, thinly sliced
1 ½ pounds sirloin or top round
   steak, about 1 inch thick
1 tablespoon Worcestershire sauce
2 tablespoons wholegrain mustard
2 tablespoons water
salt and pepper

method

1 Spread each slice of bread with some butter and add a
   few salad leaves to the bottom slices.

2 Heat 2 tablespoons of the oil in a large, heavy-bottom
   skillet over a medium heat. Add the onions and cook,
   stirring occasionally, for 10–15 minutes until softened
   and golden brown. Using a slotted spoon, transfer to
   plate and set aside.

3 Increase the heat to high and add the remaining
   oil to the pan. Add the steak, season to taste with
   pepper, and cook quickly on both sides to seal. Red
   the heat to medium and cook, turning once, for
   2½–3 minutes each side for rare or 3½–5 minutes e
   side for medium. Transfer the steak to a plate.

4 Add the Worcestershire sauce, mustard, and water
   the pan and stir to deglaze by scraping any sedim
   from the base of the pan. Return the onions to the
   season to taste with salt and pepper, mix well.

5 Thinly slice the steak across the grain, divide betwe
   the four bottom slices of bread, and cover with the
   onions. Cover with the top slices of bread and pre
   down gently. Serve immediately.

ham & cheese sandwich

ingredients

makes 1 sandwich

2 slices country-style bread,
    such as white Italian bread,
    thinly sliced

2 tablespoons butter, at room
    temperature

½ cup shredded Gruyère cheese

1 slice cooked ham, trimmed to fit
    the bread, if necessary

method

1 Thinly spread each slice of bread on one side with
  butter, then put one slice on the work surface, butter
  side down. Sprinkle half the cheese over it, to the ed
  of the bread, then add the ham and top with the
  remaining cheese. Add the other slice of bread,
  buttered side up, and press down.

2 Heat a heavy-bottom skillet, ideally nonstick,
  over a medium–high heat until hot. Reduce the he
  to medium, add the sandwich and fry on one side
  2–3 minutes, until golden brown.

3 Flip the sandwich over and fry on the other side fo
  2–3 minutes, until all the cheese is melted and the
  bread is golden brown. Cut the sandwich in half
  diagonally and serve immediately.

tuna melt

ingredients

makes 4 melts

4 slices sourdough bread

14 ounces canned tuna,
drained and flaked

4 tablespoons mayonnaise,
or to taste

1 tablespoon Dijon mustard or
wholegrain mustard,
plus extra, to taste

4 scallions, chopped

2 tablespoons dill pickle or sweet
pickle, to taste

1 hard-boiled egg, shelled and
finely chopped

1 small carrot, grated

1 tablespoon capers in brine,
rinsed and roughly chopped

2 tablespoons chopped fresh
parsley or chives

handful of lettuce leaves

8 thin slices cheddar cheese

salt and pepper

method

1 Preheat the broiler to high and position the broi
about 4 inches from the heat source. Line a baki
sheet with foil and set aside. Place the bread
on the broiler rack and toast for 2 minutes on ea
or until crisp and lightly browned.

2 Meanwhile, put the tuna in a bowl with the
mayonnaise and mustard and beat together to
break up the tuna. Add the scallions, pickle, egg
carrot, capers, and salt and pepper to taste and
together, adding extra mayonnaise or mustard t
Stir in the parsley.

3 Put the toast on the foil-lined baking sheet and
each slice with a lettuce leaf. Divide the tuna sa
between the slices of toast and spread out. Top
melt with cheese slices, cut to fit.

4 Place under the broiler and broil for 2 minutes, c
the cheese is melted and very lightly browned.
to a plate and serve immediately.

pasta with pesto

ingredients

serves 4

1 pound dried tagliatelle
salt
fresh basil leaves, to garnish

pesto

2 garlic cloves
¼ cup pine nuts
2½ cups fresh basil leaves
½ cup freshly grated Parmesan
  cheese
½ cup olive oil
salt

method

1 To make the pesto, put the garlic, pine nuts, a large
  pinch of salt, and the basil into a mortar and pound
  paste with a pestle. Transfer to a bowl and gradually
  work in the cheese with a wooden spoon, then add
  olive oil to make a thick, creamy sauce. Taste and ad
  the seasoning, if necessary.

2 Alternatively, put the garlic, pine nuts, and a large p
  of salt into a blender or food processor and process
  briefly. Add the basil and process to a paste. With th
  motor still running, gradually add the olive oil. Scra
  into a bowl and beat in the cheese. Taste and adjus
  seasoning, if necessary.

3 Bring a large saucepan of lightly salted water to a b
  Add the pasta, bring back to a boil, and cook for
  8–10 minutes, or until tender but still firm to the b.

4 Drain well, return to the saucepan, and toss with h
  the pesto, then divide between warmed serving pl
  and top with the remaining pesto. Garnish with the
  basil leaves and serve.

macaroni & cheese

ingredients

serves 4

9 ounces dried macaroni
½ stick butter, plus extra for
    cooking the pasta
2½ cups milk
½ teaspoon grated nutmeg
scant ¼ cup all-purpose flour
1¾ cups shredded sharp cheddar
    cheese
½ cup freshly grated Parmesan
    cheese
6½ cups baby spinach
salt and pepper

method

1 Cook the macaroni according to the instructions on t
packet. Remove from the heat, drain, add a small pat
butter to keep it soft, return to the saucepan, and cov
to keep warm.

2 Put the milk and nutmeg into a saucepan over a low
heat. Heat until warm, but don't boil. Melt the butter
a separate heavy-bottom saucepan over a low heat.
Add the flour and stir to make a paste. Cook gently fc
2 minutes. Add the milk a little at a time, whisking it
into the paste, then cook for about 10–15 minutes to
make a smooth sauce.

3 Add three-quarters of the cheddar cheese and
Parmesan cheese and stir through until they have
melted in. Add the spinach, season to taste with salt
and pepper, and remove from the heat.

4 Preheat the broiler to high. Put the macaroni into a
shallow ovenproof dish, then pour the sauce over t
Scatter the remaining cheese on top and place the
dish under the preheated broiler. Broil until the che
begins to brown, then serve immediately.

spaghetti bolognese

ingredients

serves 4

1 tablespoon olive oil
1 onion, finely chopped
2 garlic cloves, chopped
1 carrot, chopped
1 celery stalk, chopped
1¾ ounces pancetta or bacon, diced
12 ounces fresh lean ground beef
1 (14 ½-ounce) can diced tomatoes
2 teaspoons dried oregano
½ cup red wine
2 tablespoons tomato paste
12 ounces dried spaghetti
salt and pepper
chopped fresh parsley, to garnish

method

1 Heat the oil in a large skillet. Add the onion and coo for 3 minutes. Add the garlic, carrot, celery, and pancetta and sauté for 3–4 minutes, or until just beginning to brown.

2 Add the beef and cook over a high heat for another 3 minutes or until all of the meat is browned. Stir in the tomatoes, oregano, and wine and bring to a boil. Reduce the heat, cover, and leave to simmer fo about 45 minutes.

3 Stir in the tomato paste and season to taste with sa and pepper.

4 Bring a large saucepan of lightly salted water to a b Add the pasta, bring back to a boil, and cook for 8–10 minutes, until tender but still firm to the bite. Drain thoroughly.

5 Transfer the spaghetti to serving plates and pour o the bolognese sauce. Toss to mix well, garnish with parsley, and serve hot.

mushroom bruschetta

ingredients

serves 4

12 slices of baguette, each
    ½ inch thick,
    or 2 individual baguettes,
    cut lengthwise
3 tablespoons olive oil
2 garlic cloves, crushed
3 cups cremini mushrooms, sliced
3 cups mixed wild mushrooms
2 teaspoons lemon juice
2 tablespoons chopped fresh
    parsley
salt and pepper

method

1 Preheat the broiler to medium–high. Place the slices baguette under the broiler and toast on both sides until golden. Reserve and keep warm.

2 Meanwhile, heat the oil in a skillet. Add the garlic and cook gently for a few seconds, then add the cremini mushrooms. Cook, stirring constantly, over a high he for 3 minutes. Add the wild mushrooms and cook fo an additional 2 minutes. Stir in the lemon juice.

3 Season to taste with salt and pepper and stir in the chopped parsley.

4 Spoon the mushroom mixture onto the warm toast and serve immediately.

beef with tomatoes & peas

ingredients

serves 4

½ stick butter
1 onion, finely chopped
2 carrots, finely chopped
4 tomatoes, peeled and chopped
1 tablespoon all-purpose flour
1 teaspoon mustard powder
2½ cups beef stock
1 pound 2 ounces fresh ground
    beef
6 ounces frozen peas
salt and pepper
chopped fresh parsley, to garnish

method

1 Melt the butter in a saucepan. Add the onion and carrots and cook over a low heat, stirring occasio for 5 minutes, until softened. Add the tomatoes a cook, stirring occasionally, for a further 3 minutes

2 Remove the pan from the heat and stir in the flo mustard powder. Return to the heat and cook, st constantly, for 2 minutes. Gradually stir in the sto little at a time, then bring to the boil, stirring con Cook, stirring constantly, for an additional few m until thickened.

3 Add the beef and stir to break it up. Season to ta with salt and pepper, then cover and simmer, sti occasionally, for 45 minutes.

4 Gently stir in the peas, re-cover the pan and sim. stirring occasionally, for an additional 15 minute: and adjust the seasoning, adding salt and pepp needed. Garnish with parsley and serve.

salmon-stuffed potatoes

ingredients

serves 4

4 baking potatoes,
    about 10 ounces each,
    scrubbed
9 ounces skinless salmon fillet
¾ cup soft cheese
2–3 tablespoons skim milk
2 tablespoons chopped/snipped
    fresh herbs, such as dill or
    chives
½ cup shredded sharp cheddar
    cheese
salt and pepper

method

1 Preheat the oven to 400°F. Pierce the skins of the potatoes and place on the top shelf of the preheat oven. Bake for 50–60 minutes, until the skins are cr and the centers are soft when pierced with a sharp knife or skewer.

2 Meanwhile, bring a saucepan of water to a boil, then reduce the heat until the water is simmering gently. Add the salmon fillet to the pan and cook 4–5 minutes (if in one piece), or until just cooked still moist. Using a fork, flake the flesh into a bowl.

3 In a separate bowl, blend the soft cheese with jus enough of the milk to loosen, then stir in the herb a little salt and pepper.

4 When the potatoes are cooked, preheat the broil high. Cut the potatoes in half lengthwise. Carefull scoop the potato flesh out of the skins, reserving skins. Add to the soft cheese mixture and mash together. Lightly stir in the salmon flakes.

5 Spoon the filling into the potato skins and top w the cheddar cheese. Cook under the preheated for 1–2 minutes, until the cheese is bubbling and turning golden. Serve immediately.

cauliflower cheese casserole

ingredients

serves 4

1 cauliflower, trimmed and cut into
   florets (1½ pounds prepared
   weight)
3 tablespoons butter
⅓ cup all-purpose flour
2 cups milk
1 cup finely shredded cheddar
   cheese
whole nutmeg, for grating
1 tablespoon grated Parmesan
   cheese
salt and pepper

method

1 Bring a saucepan of lightly salted water to a boil, a
   the cauliflower, bring back to a boil, and cook for
   4–5 minutes. It should still be firm. Drain, place in a
   warm 1½ pint–1 quart gratin dish, and keep warm

2 Melt the butter in the rinsed-out pan over a mediu
   heat and stir in the flour. Cook for 1 minute, stirring
   constantly.

3 Remove the pan from the heat and gradually stir i
   milk until you have a smooth consistency.

4 Return the pan to a low heat and continue to stir
   the sauce comes to a boil and thickens. Reduce th
   heat and simmer gently, stirring constantly, for ab
   3 minutes, until the sauce is creamy and smooth.

5 Remove from the heat and stir in the cheddar che
   and a good grating of the nutmeg. Taste and seas
   well with salt and pepper. Meanwhile, preheat the
   broiler to high.

6 Pour the hot sauce over the cauliflower, top with t
   Parmesan cheese and place under the preheated
   broiler to brown. Serve immediately.

macaroni salad

ingredients

serves 6–8

8 ounces dried macaroni
4 tablespoons mayonnaise,
    plus extra if needed
4 tablespoons natural yogurt
1 tablespoon fresh lemon juice
½ teaspoon garlic salt
½ teaspoon pepper
⅓ cup diced celery
⅓ cup finely chopped scallions
⅓ cup finely chopped black olives
1¼ cups finely chopped tomatoes
2 tablespoons chopped fresh
    flat-leaf parsley
salt and pepper

method

1 Bring a medium-sized saucepan of lightly salted water to a boil, add the macaroni and cook according to the packet instructions. Drain.

2 Meanwhile, combine the mayonnaise, yogurt, lemon juice, garlic salt, and the pepper in a large bowl. Stir in the hot macaroni, then add the celery, scallions, olives, tomatoes, and parsley. Season to taste with salt and pepper and add more mayonnaise if it seems dry, then leave to cool completely.

3 Cover with plastic wrap and chill for at least 2 hours until cold. Serve cold. The salad will keep in the refrigerator for up to 3 days.

corned beef hash

ingredients

serves 6

2 tablespoons butter
1 tablespoon vegetable oil
1½ pounds corned beef,
    cut into small cubes
1 onion, diced
4½ cups potatoes,
    cut into small cubes
¼ teaspoon paprika
¼ teaspoon garlic powder
4 tablespoons diced green bell
    pepper or jalapeño chilies
1 tablespoon snipped chives,
    plus extra to garnish
salt and pepper
6 poached eggs, to serve

method

1 Put the butter, oil, corned beef, and onion into a large, cold, nonstick or heavy-bottom skillet. Place the pan over a medium–low heat and cook, stirring occasionally, for 10 minutes.

2 Meanwhile, bring a large saucepan of lightly salted water to a boil, add the potatoes, bring back to a boil and cook for 5–7 minutes, until partially cooked but very firm. Drain well and add to the skillet, together with the remaining ingredients.

3 Mix together well and press down lightly with a spatula to flatten. Increase the heat to medium. Every 10 minutes, turn the mixture with a spatula to bring the crusty base up to the top. Do this several times until the mixture is well-browned, the potatoes are crisp-edged, and the cubes of meat are caramelized.

4 Taste and adjust the seasoning, if necessary. Transfer to warmed plates and top each with a poached egg. Garnish with chives and serve immediately.

fried chicken wings

ingredients

serves 4

12 chicken wings
1 egg
¼ cup milk
4 heaped tablespoons all-purpose
   flour
1 teaspoon paprika
2 cups breadcrumbs
4 tablespoons butter
salt and pepper

method

1 Preheat the oven to 425°F. Separate the chicken wing
   into three pieces each. Discard the bony tip. Beat the
   egg with the milk in a shallow dish. Combine the flou
   paprika, and salt and pepper to taste in a separate
   shallow dish. Place the breadcrumbs in another
   shallow dish.

2 Dip the chicken pieces into the egg to coat well,
   then drain and roll in the seasoned flour. Remove,
   shaking off any excess, then roll the chicken in the
   breadcrumbs, gently pressing them onto the surfac
   and shaking off any excess.

3 Put the butter in a shallow roasting pan large enou
   to hold all the chicken pieces in a single layer. Place
   pan in the preheated oven and melt the butter.
   Remove from the oven and arrange the chicken,
   skin-side down, in the pan. Return to the oven and
   bake for 10 minutes. Turn and bake for an addition
   10 minutes, or until the chicken is tender and the j
   run clear when a skewer is inserted into the thicke
   part of the meat.

4 Remove the chicken from the pan. Serve hot or at
   room temperature.

tuna fish hash

ingredients

serves 4

2 cooked potatoes, diced
1 pound canned fish, such as tuna,
    drained and flaked,
    or 12 ounces leftover cooked
    fish, flaked
½ stick butter
3 tablespoons light cream or milk
salt and pepper
chopped fresh parsley, to garnish

method

1 Gently mix together the potatoes and fish in a bowl, and season to taste with salt and pepper.

2 Melt the butter in a heavy-bottom skillet over a medium–low heat. Add the fish mixture and spread it out evenly, pressing down with a spatula to crush t potatoes slightly. Pour the cream over the top and cook, occasionally shaking the skillet, for about 10 minutes, until the underside is golden.

3 Invert a plate over the skillet, then, holding the plate and skillet together, turn the hash onto the plate. Carefully slide it back into the skillet and cook for an additional 5–8 minutes, until the second side is gold Garnish with parsley and serve immediately.

potato pancakes

ingredients

makes 12 pancakes

4 large potatoes, peeled and coarsely grated
1 large onion, grated
2 eggs, lightly beaten
⅓ cup fine matzo meal
1 teaspoon salt
pepper
sunflower oil, for frying

to serve

sour cream
thinly sliced smoked salmon
snipped chives

method

1 Preheat the oven to 225°F and line an ovenproof plate with paper towels. Working in small batches, put the potatoes on a dish towel, fold over and squeeze to extract as much water as possible.

2 Put the potatoes in a large bowl, add the onion, eggs, matzo meal, and the salt. Add pepper to taste and mix together.

3 Heat a large, heavy-bottom skillet over a medium–high heat. Add a thin layer of oil and heat until hot. Drop 2 tablespoons of the batter into the pan and flatten slightly. Add as many more pancakes as will fit without overcrowding the pan. Fry for 2 minutes, or until crisp and golden underneath. Flip or turn with a spatula and continue frying for an additional 1–2 minutes, until crisp and golden.

4 Repeat this process using the remaining batter, add extra oil between batches, if necessary. Keep the cooked pancakes warm in the preheated oven.

5 Serve the pancakes hot, topped with sour cream and smoked salmon and sprinkled with chives.

variation

For a special treat, add a small spoonful of caviar or lumpfish roe on top of the cream instead of the salmon

fabulous
family food

barbecue-glazed drumsticks

ingredients

serves 6

12 chicken drumsticks,
about 3½ pounds
1 cup barbecue sauce
1 tablespoon light brown sugar
1 tablespoon cider vinegar
1 teaspoon salt
½ teaspoon pepper
½ teaspoon hot pepper sauce
vegetable oil, for brushing

method

1 Using a sharp knife, make two slashes, about 1 inch apart, into the thickest part of the drumsticks, cutting to the bone. Put the drumsticks into a large, sealable plastic freezer bag.

2 Mix together 4 tablespoons of the barbecue sauce, sugar, vinegar, salt, pepper, and hot pepper sauce in a small bowl. Pour the mixture into the bag, press out most of the air and seal tightly. Shake the bag gently distribute the sauce evenly and leave to marinate in t refrigerator for at least 4 hours.

3 Preheat the oven to 400°F. Line a baking sheet with f and brush lightly with oil.

4 Using tongs, transfer the drumsticks to the prepared baking sheet, spacing them evenly apart. Discard the marinade. Brush both sides of the drumsticks with some of the remaining barbecue sauce.

5 Bake in the preheated oven for 15 minutes, then remove from the oven and brush generously with more barbecue sauce. Return to the oven and repea this process three more times for a total cooking tin of 1 hour or until the chicken is tender and the juice run clear when a skewer is inserted into the thickes part of the meat. When done, the chicken will be cooked through with a thick, beautiful glaze.

tuna noodle casserole

ingredients

serves 4–6

7 ounces dried ribbon egg pasta, such as tagliatelle
2 tablespoons butter
1 cup fine fresh breadcrumbs
1¾ cups canned condensed cream of mushroom soup
½ cup milk
2 celery stalks, chopped
1 red bell pepper, deseeded and chopped
1 green bell pepper, deseeded and chopped
1¼ cups coarsely shredded cheddar cheese
2 tablespoons chopped fresh parsley
7 ounces canned tuna in oil, drained and flaked
salt and pepper

method

1 Preheat the oven to 400°F. Bring a large saucepan of lightly salted water to a boil. Add the pasta, bring back to a boil and cook for 2 minutes less than specified on the packet instructions.

2 Meanwhile, melt the butter in a separate small saucepan. Stir in the breadcrumbs, then remove from the heat and set aside.

3 Drain the pasta well and set aside. Pour the soup into the pasta pan, set over a medium heat, then stir in the milk, celery, red bell pepper, green bell pepper, half the cheese, and all the parsley.

4 Add the tuna and gently stir in so that the flakes don't break up. Season to taste with salt and pepper. Heat just until small bubbles appear around the edge of mixture—do not boil.

5 Stir the pasta into the pan and use two forks to mix the ingredients together. Spoon the mixture into an ovenproof dish that also is suitable for serving, and spread it out.

6 Stir the remaining cheese into the buttered breadcrumbs, then sprinkle over the top of the pasta mix. Bake in the preheated oven for 20–25 minutes, until the topping is golden. Remove from the oven, then leave to stand for 5 minutes before serving straight from the dish.

chicken pot pies

ingredients

serves 6

1 tablespoon olive oil

3¼ cups sliced button mushrooms

1 onion, finely chopped

2 cups sliced carrots

1 cup sliced celery

4 cups chicken stock

¾ stick butter

½ cup all-purpose flour, plus extra for dusting

2 pounds skinless, boneless chicken breasts, cut into 1-inch cubes

1 cup frozen peas

1 teaspoon chopped fresh thyme or a pinch of dried thyme

1½ pounds prepared pastry dough, thawed, if frozen

1 egg, lightly beaten

salt and pepper

method

1 Heat the oil in a large saucepan and fry the mushroo and onion gently until golden. Add the carrots, celery and half the stock and simmer for 12–15 minutes, un the vegetables are almost tender.

2 Melt the butter in another large saucepan over a medium heat. Whisk in the flour and cook, stirring constantly, for 4 minutes. Gradually whisk in the remaining chicken stock. Reduce the heat and simm stirring, until thickened.

3 Stir in the vegetables, chicken, peas, and thyme, and season with salt and pepper. Simmer, stirring constantly, for 5 minutes. Adjust the seasoning, if necessary, and remove from the heat. Preheat the oven to 400°F.

4 Divide the filling between six large ramekins, leavin ½ inch at the top. Roll out the pastry on a lightly floured work surface and cut out six rounds slightly larger than the ramekins. Put the rounds on top an fold over all the way around to make a rim. Cut a sn cross in the center of each.

5 Put the ramekins on a baking sheet and brush the pastry tops with the beaten egg. Bake in the prehe oven for 35–40 minutes, until golden brown and bubbling. Remove from the oven and leave to coc 15 minutes before serving.

crab cakes with tartare sauce

ingredients

makes 6 cakes

1 extra-large egg, beaten
2 tablespoons mayonnaise
½ teaspoon Dijon mustard
¼ teaspoon Worcestershire sauce
½ teaspoon Old Bay seasoning
¼ teaspoon salt
pinch of cayenne pepper (optional)
10 saltine crackers, finely crushed
1 pound fresh crabmeat
⅓–¾ cup fresh breadcrumbs
2 tablespoons unsalted butter
1 tablespoon vegetable oil
salad leaves and lemon wedges,
    to serve

tartare sauce

1 cup mayonnaise
4 tablespoons sweet pickle relish
1 tablespoon very finely chopped
    onion
1 tablespoon chopped capers
1 tablespoon chopped parsley
1½ tablespoons freshly squeezed
    lemon juice
dash of Worcestershire sauce
few drops of hot pepper sauce
    (optional)
salt and pepper

method

1 To make the crab cakes, whisk together the egg, mayonnaise, mustard, Worcestershire sauce, Old Bay seasoning, salt, and cayenne pepper, if using, in a large bowl until combined. Stir in the cracker crumbs with a spatula, then leave to stand for 5 minutes.

2 Pick over the crabmeat to remove any pieces of shell, then gently fold into the mixture, trying to avoid breaking it up too much. Cover the bowl with plastic wrap and chill in the refrigerator for at least 1 hour.

3 Meanwhile, make the tartare sauce. Mix together all the ingredients in a bowl and season to taste with salt and pepper. Cover and chill in the refrigerator for at least 1 hour before serving.

4 Sprinkle the breadcrumbs over a large plate until lightly covered. Shape the crab mixture into six even-sized cakes, about 1 inch thick, placing them on the plate as they are formed. Dust the tops of each crab cake lightly with more breadcrumbs.

5 Melt the butter with the oil in a large skillet over a medium–high heat. Carefully transfer each crab cake from the plate to the pan using a metal spatula.

6 Cook the crab cakes for 4 minutes on each side, until golden brown. Remove from the pan and drain on paper towels. Serve immediately with the tartare sauce, salad leaves, and lemon wedges.

pizza

ingredients

serves 6

pizza dough

4½ teaspoons active dry yeast
1 teaspoon sugar
1 cup lukewarm water
2¾ cups white bread flour,
    plus extra for dusting
1 teaspoon salt
1 tablespoon olive oil, plus extra
    for oiling

topping

1 (14½- ounce) can diced
    tomatoes
2 garlic cloves, crushed
2 teaspoons dried basil
1 tablespoon olive oil
2 tablespoons tomato paste
1 cup diced mozzarella cheese
2 tablespoons freshly grated
    Parmesan cheese
salt and pepper
fresh basil leaves, to garnish

method

1 Place the yeast and sugar in a measuring jug and mix with 4 tablespoons of the water. Leave the yeast mixture in a warm place for 15 minutes or until frothy.

2 Sift together the flour and salt in a bowl and make a well in the center. Add the oil, the yeast mixture, and the remaining water. Using a wooden spoon, mix to form a smooth dough. Place the dough onto a floured work surface and knead for 4–5 minutes or until smooth. Return the dough to the bowl, cover with a sheet of oiled plastic wrap, and leave to rise for 30 minutes, or until doubled in size.

3 Knead the dough for 2 minutes. Stretch the dough with your hands or roll out on a floured surface with rolling pin, then place it on an oiled baking sheet. The dough should be no more than ¼ inch thick.

4 Preheat the oven to 400°F. To make the topping, place the tomatoes, garlic, basil, oil, and salt and pepper to taste in a large skillet over a medium heat and leave to simmer for 20 minutes or until the sauce has thickened. Stir in the tomato paste and leave to cool slightly.

5 Spread the topping evenly over the pizza base. Top with the mozzarella cheese and Parmesan cheese, bake in the preheated oven for 20–25 minutes. Serve hot, garnished with basil leaves.

salmon croquettes

ingredients

serves 4

1 pound starchy potatoes,
   cut into chunks
1 pound mixed fish fillets, such as
   salmon or cod, skinned
2 tablespoons chopped fresh
   tarragon
grated rind of 1 lemon
2 tablespoons heavy cream
1 tablespoon all-purpose flour
1 egg, beaten
2½ cups breadcrumbs, made from
   day-old white or wholemeal
   bread
4 tablespoons vegetable oil,
   for shallow-frying
salt and pepper
watercress and lemon wedges,
   to serve

method

1 Cook the potatoes in a large saucepan of boiling salted water for 15–20 minutes. Drain well and mash with a potato masher until smooth.

2 Meanwhile, put the fish in a skillet and just cover with water. Place over a medium heat and bring to a boil, then reduce the heat, cover, and simmer gently for 5 minutes, until cooked.

3 Remove from the heat and drain the fish onto a plate. When cool enough to handle, flake the fish into large chunks, making sure that there are no bones.

4 Mix the potatoes with the fish, tarragon, lemon rind, and cream. Season well with salt and pepper and shape into 4 large patties or 8 smaller ones.

5 Dust the patties with flour and dip them into the beaten egg. Coat thoroughly in the breadcrumbs. Place on a baking tray and leave to chill in the refrigerator at least 30 minutes.

6 Heat the oil in the clean skillet and fry the patties over medium heat for 5 minutes on each side, turning them carefully using a spatula.

7 Serve with the watercress, accompanied by lemon wedges for squeezing over the fish cakes.

roasted butternut squash

ingredients

serves 4

1 butternut squash,
about 1 pound
1 onion, chopped
2–3 garlic cloves, crushed
4 small tomatoes, chopped
1⅓ cups cremini mushrooms,
chopped
3 ounces canned lima beans,
drained, rinsed, and roughly
chopped
1 zucchini, about 4 ounces, grated
1 tablespoon chopped fresh
oregano, plus extra, to garnish
2 tablespoons tomato paste
1¼ cups water
4 scallions, chopped
1 teaspoon Worcestershire sauce,
or to taste
pepper

method

1 Preheat the oven to 375°F. Pierce the squash all over
with a metal skewer then roast for 40 minutes, or until
tender. Remove from the oven and leave to rest until
cool enough to handle.

2 Cut the squash in half, scoop out and discard the seed
then scoop out some of the flesh, making hollows in
both halves. Chop the scooped-out flesh and put in a
bowl. Place the two squash halves side by side in a
large roasting pan.

3 Add the onion, garlic, tomatoes, and mushrooms to
the squash flesh in the bowl. Add the lima beans,
zucchini, oregano, and pepper to taste and mix well.
Spoon the filling into the two halves of the squash,
packing it down as firmly as possible.

4 Mix the tomato paste with the water, scallions, and
Worcestershire sauce in a small bowl and pour over
the squash.

5 Cover loosely with a large sheet of foil and bake for
30 minutes, or until piping hot. Serve in warmed bo
garnished with some chopped oregano.

meatloaf

ingredients

serves 6–8

½ cup diced carrots
½ cup diced celery
1 onion, diced
1 red bell pepper, seeded and chopped
4 large white mushrooms, sliced
2 tablespoons butter
1 tablespoon olive oil, plus extra for brushing
3 garlic cloves, crushed
1 teaspoon dried thyme
2 teaspoons finely chopped rosemary
1 teaspoon Worcestershire sauce
4 tablespoons ketchup
½ teaspoon cayenne pepper
2½ pounds ground beef, chilled
2 teaspoons salt
1 teaspoon pepper
2 eggs, beaten
1 cup fresh breadcrumbs
green peas and mashed potatoes (see page 102), to serve

glaze

2 tablespoons brown sugar
2 tablespoons ketchup
1 tablespoon Dijon mustard
salt

method

1 Put the vegetables into a food processor and pulse until very finely chopped. Melt the butter with the oil and garlic in a large skillet. Add the vegetable mixture and cook over a medium heat, stirring frequently, for about 10 minutes. Remove the pan from the heat and stir in the thyme, rosemary, Worcestershire sauce, ketchup, and cayenne pepper. Leave to cool to room temperature.

2 Preheat the oven to 325°F. Lightly brush a shallow roasting pan with olive oil.

3 Put the beef into a large bowl and gently break it up with your fingertips. Add the cooled vegetable mixture, salt, pepper, and eggs and mix gently. Add the breadcrumbs and mix to combine. The less you work the meat, the better the final texture.

4 Put the meatloaf mixture in the center of the prepared roasting pan and shape it into a loaf about 6 inches wide by 4 inches high. Bake in the preheated oven for 30 minutes.

5 To make the glaze, whisk together all the ingredients with a pinch of salt in a small bowl.

6 Remove the meatloaf from the oven and spread the glaze over the top and sides. Bake for an additional 15 minutes. Slice thickly and serve with peas and m

spaghetti & meatballs

ingredients

serves 4

2 tablespoons olive oil, plus extra for brushing

1 onion, finely diced

4 garlic cloves, finely chopped

½ teaspoon dried Italian herbs

2 cups fresh fine breadcrumbs

4 tablespoons milk

2 pounds ground beef, well chilled

2 extra-large eggs, lightly beaten

5 tablespoons chopped fresh flat-leaf parsley

¾ cup freshly grated Parmesan cheese, plus extra to serve

6 cups marinara or other pasta sauce

1 cup water

1 pound thick dried spaghetti

salt and pepper

method

1 Heat the oil in a saucepan and gently cook the onion, garlic, and a pinch of salt for 6–7 minutes until soften and golden. Remove from the heat, stir in the herbs, and leave to cool.

2 Put the breadcrumbs into a bowl, toss with the milk, and leave to soak for 10 minutes. Preheat the oven to 425°F. Brush a baking sheet with oil.

3 Put the beef, eggs, parsley, cheese, breadcrumbs, cooled onion mixture, and salt and pepper to taste into a bowl. Mix well with your hands until thoroughly combined.

4 Roll the mixture into balls about the size of a golf ba Put them on the prepared baking sheet and bake in the oven for 20 minutes. Heat the pasta sauce and t water in a saucepan. When the meatballs are done, them to the hot sauce, reduce the heat to very low, cover, and simmer gently for 45 minutes.

5 Cook the spaghetti according to the packet instructions, until tender but still firm to the bite. D in a colander and pour into a large serving dish. Lac some of the sauce from the meatballs over it and t to coat. Top with the meatballs and the remaining sauce, sprinkle with cheese, and serve immediately

hamburgers

ingredients

makes 6 burgers

2¼ pounds ground beef
1 small onion, grated
1 tablespoon chopped fresh
    parsley
2 teaspoons Worcestershire sauce
2 tablespoons sunflower oil
salt and pepper

to serve

6 burger buns, split and toasted
lettuce leaves
tomato slices
dill pickles, sliced
ketchup

method

1 Put the beef, onion, and parsley into a bowl and add
the Worcestershire sauce. Season to taste with salt
and pepper, and mix well with your hands until
thoroughly combined.

2 Divide the mixture into six equal portions and shape
into balls, then gently flatten into patties. If you have
time, chill in the refrigerator for 30 minutes to firm up.

3 Heat the oil in a large skillet. Add the burgers, in
batches, and cook over a medium heat for 5–8 minu
on each side, turning them carefully with a spatula.
Remove from the pan and keep warm while you coo
the remaining burgers.

4 Serve in toasted buns with lettuce leaves, tomato
slices, dill pickles, and ketchup.

meat lasagne

ingredients

serves 6

2 tablespoons olive oil
1 pound 2 ounces ground beef
1 onion, chopped
1 garlic clove, finely chopped
1 carrot, diced
1 tablespoon chopped fresh
    flat-leaf parsley
6 fresh basil leaves, torn
2½ cups tomato purée
2¼ cups ricotta cheese
1 egg, lightly beaten
8 oven-ready lasagne sheets
2 cups mozzarella cheese,
    shredded
salt and pepper

method

1 Heat the oil in a saucepan. Add the beef, onion, garlic, and carrot, and cook over a medium heat, stirring frequently and breaking up the meat with a wooden spoon, for 5–8 minutes, until the beef is evenly browned.

2 Stir in the herbs, season to taste with salt and peppe and pour in the tomato purée. Bring to a boil, then reduce the heat, cover and simmer for 15 minutes.

3 Meanwhile, preheat the oven to 375°F. Mix the ricotta with the egg, stirring until smooth and thoroughly combined.

4 Make alternating layers of the beef mixture, lasagne sheets, ricotta mixture, and mozzarella in an ovenp dish, ending with a layer of mozzarella.
Bake in the preheated oven for 40–45 minutes, unt the topping is golden and bubbling. Let stand for 5 minutes before serving.

old-fashioned chicken stew

ingredients

serves 6

2 tablespoons vegetable oil
1 whole chicken, weighng
    4-5 pounds, cut into quarters
4 cups chicken stock
4 cups water
4 garlic cloves, peeled
1 bay leaf
4 fresh thyme sprigs
5 tablespoons butter
2 carrots, cut into
    ½-inch lengths
2 celery stalks, cut into
    ½-inch lengths
1 large onion, chopped
5 tablespoons all-purpose flour
1½ teaspoons salt
pepper
dash of hot pepper sauce

dumplings

1½ cups all-purpose flour
1 teaspoon salt
2 teaspoons baking powder
¼ teaspoon baking soda
3 tablespoons butter, chilled
2 tablespoons thinly sliced
    scallions
4 tablespoons buttermilk
¾ cup milk

method

1 Heat the oil in a large casserole, add the chicken piec
and brown all over. Add the stock, water, garlic, bay l
and thyme, then cover and simmer for 30 minutes.
Remove the chicken and leave to cool. Strain the
cooking liquid and reserve, skimming off any fat.

2 Put the butter, carrots, celery, and onion into the
casserole and cook for 5 minutes. Stir in the flour an
cook, stirring constantly, for 2 minutes. Gradually wh
in the reserved cooking liquid. Add the salt, pepper,
and the hot pepper sauce. Cover and simmer for
30 minutes, until the vegetables are tender.

3 Skin the chicken pieces and tear the meat into chu
Stir the chunks into the cooked vegetables, cover t
casserole, and reduce the heat to low.

4 To make the dumplings, sift the flour, salt, baking
powder, and baking soda together into a bowl. Ru
the butter until the mixture resembles coarse
breadcrumbs. Add the scallions, buttermilk, and m
and mix into a thick dough.

5 Increase the heat under the casserole to medium
stir well. Shape the dough into large balls and add
the casserole. Cover and simmer for 15 minutes, u
the dumplings are firm and cooked in the middle.
Serve immediately.

hearty beef stew

ingredients

serves 4

3 pounds boneless chuck roast, cut into 2-inch pieces

2 tablespoons vegetable oil

2 onions, cut into 1-inch pieces

3 tablespoons all-purpose flour

3 garlic cloves, finely chopped

4 cups beef stock, plus extra if needed

3 carrots, sliced

2 celery stalks, cut into 1-inch lengths

1 tablespoon ketchup

1 bay leaf

¼ teaspoon dried thyme

¼ teaspoon dried rosemary

2 pounds Yukon gold potatoes, cut into large chunks

salt and pepper

method

1 Season the beef very generously with salt and peppe Heat the oil in a large ovenproof casserole (one that a tight-fitting lid) over a high heat. When the oil begi to smoke slightly, add the beef, in batches if necessa and cook, stirring frequently, for 5–8 minutes, until w browned. Using a slotted spoon, transfer to a bowl.

2 Reduce the heat to medium, add the onions to the casserole and cook, stirring occasionally, for 5 minut until translucent. Stir in the flour and cook, stirring constantly, for 2 minutes. Add the garlic and cook fc 1 minute. Whisk in 1 cup of the stock and cook, scraping up all the sediment from the base of the casserole, then stir in the remaining stock. Add the carrots, celery, ketchup, bay leaf, thyme, rosemary, a 1 teaspoon of salt. Return the beef to the casserole

3 Bring back to a gentle simmer, cover and cook ove low heat for 1 hour. Add the potatoes, re-cover the casserole, and simmer for an additional 30 minutes Remove the lid, increase the heat to medium and stirring occasionally, for an additional 30 minutes, until the meat and vegetables are tender.

4 If the stew becomes too thick, add a little more stc or water and adjust the seasoning, if necessary. Le stand for 15 minutes before serving.

pork chops with applesauce

ingredients

serves 4

4 pork rib chops on the bone, each
    about 1¼ inches thick,
    at room temperature
1½ tablespoons sunflower oil or
    canola oil
salt and pepper

applesauce

4 cups cooking apples, peeled,
    cored, and diced
4 tablespoons sugar, plus extra,
    if needed
finely grated zest of ½ lemon
½ tablespoon lemon juice,
    plus extra, if needed
4 tablespoons water
¼ teaspoon ground cinnamon
pat of butter

method

1 To make the applesauce, put the apples, sugar,
lemon zest, lemon juice, and water into a heavy-
bottom saucepan over a high heat and bring to a boil,
stirring to dissolve the sugar. Reduce the heat to low,
cover and simmer for 15–20 minutes, until the apples
are tender and fall apart when you mash them against
the side of the pan. Stir in the cinnamon and butter
and beat the apples until they are as smooth or chunky
as you like. Stir in extra sugar or lemon juice, to taste.
Remove the pan from the heat, cover, and keep the
apple sauce warm.

2 Meanwhile, preheat the oven to 400°F. Pat the chops
dry and season to taste with salt and pepper. Heat the
oil in a large ovenproof skillet over a medium–high
heat. Add the chops and fry for 3 minutes on each side
to brown.

3 Transfer the pan to the oven and roast the chops
for 7–9 minutes until cooked through and the juices
run clear when you cut them. Remove the pan from
the oven, cover with foil and let stand for 3 minutes.
Gently reheat the applesauce, if necessary.

4 Transfer the chops to warmed plates and spoon over
the pan juices. Serve immediately, accompanied by
applesauce.

steak & fries

ingredients

serves 4

4 porterhouse steaks,
    about 8 ounces each
4 teaspoons hot pepper sauce
salt and pepper

fries

2 large potatoes, about 1 pound
2 tablespoons sunflower oil

watercress butter

1 bunch of watercress
¾ stick unsalted butter, softened

method

1 To make the fries, preheat the oven to 400°F. Cut the potatoes into thick, even-sized fries. Rinse them under cold running water and then dry well on a clean dish towel. Place in a bowl, add the oil and toss together until coated.

2 Spread the fries on a baking sheet and cook in the preheated oven for 40–45 minutes, turning once, until golden.

3 To make the watercress butter, finely chop enough watercress to fill 4 tablespoons. Place the butter in a small bowl and beat in the chopped watercress with fork until fully incorporated. Cover with plastic wrap and leave to chill in the refrigerator until required.

4 Preheat a griddle pan to high. Sprinkle each steak w 1 teaspoon of the hot pepper sauce, rubbing it in w Season to taste with salt and pepper.

5 Cook the steaks in the preheated pan for 2½ minute each side for rare, 4 minutes each side for medium, 6 minutes each side for well done. Transfer to servir plates and serve immediately, topped with the watercress butter and accompanied by the fries.

turkey & stuffing

ingredients
serves 8–10

10-pound oven-ready turkey,
    wiped and patted dry
2 garlic cloves, sliced
1 orange, sliced
4 tablespoons butter, melted,
    for brushing
salt and pepper

stuffing

1 pound spicy bulk sausage
4 tablespoons butter, plus extra for
    greasing
3 celery stalks, finely chopped
1 onion, finely chopped
6 slices day-old bread, crusts
    removed and cubed
½ cup turkey stock or vegetable
    stock, plus extra if needed
1 cup dried fruit, such as currants
    and raisins
1¼ cups coarsely chopped fresh
    cranberries
¼ cup finely chopped fresh parsley
2 teaspoons dried thyme
1 teaspoon dried sage
finely grated zest and juice of
    2 large oranges
salt and pepper

method

1 To make the stuffing, put the sausage into a skillet over a medium–high heat and cook until browned. Remove the meat and pour off the fat. Melt the butter in the pan, add the celery and onion and fry, stirring, until softened. Add the bread and stir until it starts to color, then add the contents of the pan to the sausage. Stir in the stock, dried fruit, cranberries, herbs, and orange zest. Add enough orange juice to make a moist stuffing and season to taste.

2 Preheat the oven to 350°F. Use enough stuffing to fill the neck end of the turkey, securing the skin with wooden toothpicks. Put the garlic and orange slices into the cavity and truss the legs together. Put any leftover stuffing in a greased oven dish and cover with foil.

3 Weigh the stuffed bird and calculate the cooking time at 20 minutes per 1 pound, plus 20 minutes. Place the bird, breast side up, on a roasting rack in a roasting pan, smear with butter, and season to taste with salt and pepper. Cover loosely with foil and roast for the calculated time, or until the juices run clear when a skewer is inserted into the thickest part of the meat.

4 Remove the turkey from the oven, cover and let rest for 30–45 minutes. Roast the extra stuffing for 20–25 minutes. Carve the turkey and serve with the stuffing.

baked ham

ingredients

serves 6

3 pound boneless ham
2 tablespoons Dijon mustard
scant ½ cup brown sugar
½ teaspoon ground cinnamon
½ teaspoon ground ginger
18 whole cloves
prepared orange and red-currant
    sauce, to serve

method

1 Place the ham in a large saucepan, cover with cold water, and slowly bring to a boil over a gentle heat. Cover the pan and simmer very gently for 1 hour.

2 Preheat the oven to 400°F.

3 Remove the ham from the pan and drain. Remove the rind from the ham and discard. Score the fat into a diamond-shaped pattern with a sharp knife.

4 Spread the mustard over the fat. Mix the sugar and the ground spices together on a large plate and roll the ham in the mixture, pressing down well to coat even

5 Stud the diamond shapes with cloves and place the ham in a roasting pan. Roast in the preheated oven f 20 minutes, until the glaze is a rich golden color.

6 To serve hot, let stand for 20 minutes before carving. the ham is to be served cold, it can be cooked a day ahead. Serve with the orange and red-currant sauce

leg of lamb pot roast

ingredients

serves 4

1 leg of lamb, weighing 3½
    pounds
3–4 fresh rosemary sprigs
4 ounces bacon strips
    (about 4–6 strips)
4 tablespoons olive oil
2–3 garlic cloves, crushed
2 onions, sliced
2 carrots, sliced
2 celery stalks, sliced
1¼ cups dry white wine
1 tablespoon tomato paste
1¼ cups lamb stock or chicken
    stock
3 tomatoes, peeled, quartered,
    and seeded
1 tablespoon chopped fresh
    parsley
1 tablespoon chopped fresh
    oregano or marjoram
salt and pepper
fresh rosemary sprigs, to garnish

method

1 Wipe the lamb all over with paper towels, trim off any
   excess fat, and season to taste with salt and pepper,
   rubbing in well. Lay the sprigs of rosemary over the
   lamb, cover evenly with the bacon, and tie in place
   securely with some kitchen string.

2 Heat the oil in a large skillet over a medium heat, add
   the lamb and fry for 10 minutes, turning several times.
   Remove from the pan.

3 Preheat the oven to 325°F. Transfer the oil from the pan
   to a large, ovenproof casserole. Add the garlic and
   onions, and cook for 3–4 minutes, until the onions are
   beginning to soften. Add the carrots and celery, and
   cook for an additional few minutes.

4 Lay the lamb on top of the vegetables. Pour the wine
   over the lamb, add the tomato paste, and simmer for
   3–4 minutes. Add the stock, tomatoes, and herbs, and
   season to taste with salt and pepper. Bring back to a
   boil and cook for a further 3–4 minutes.

5 Lightly cover the casserole and cook in the preheated
   oven for 2–2½ hours, until very tender.

6 Remove the lamb from the casserole and keep warm.
   Strain the juices, skimming off any fat. Garnish the
   with sprigs of rosemary and serve with the vegetables
   and juices.

roast chicken

ingredients

serves 6

1 whole chicken, weighing about
5 pounds
4 tablespoons butter
2 tablespoons chopped fresh
lemon thyme
1 lemon, quartered
½ cup dry white wine, plus extra if
needed
salt and pepper
roasted vegetables, to serve

method

1 Preheat the oven to 425°F. Make sure the chicken
clean, wiping it inside and out with paper towel,
place in a roasting pan.

2 In a bowl, soften the butter with a fork, mix in the
thyme, and season well with salt and pepper. Spr
the chicken all over with the herb butter, inside a
out, and place the lemon pieces inside the body
Pour the wine over the chicken.

3 Roast in the center of the preheated oven for
20 minutes. Reduce the temperature to 375°F an
continue to roast for an additional 1¼ hours, bast
frequently. Cover with foil if the skin begins to bro
too much. If the liquid in the pan dries out, add a
more wine or water.

4 Test that the chicken is cooked by piercing the th
part of the leg with a sharp knife and making sure
juices run clear. Remove from the oven.

5 Place the chicken on a warmed serving plate, cov
with foil and let rest for 10 minutes before carving

6 Place the roasting pan on the stove and bubble t
pan juices gently over a low heat, until they have
reduced and are thick and glossy. Season to taste
with salt and pepper. Serve the chicken with the
juices and roasted vegetables.

roast beef

ingredients

serves 6

olive oil, for rubbing
6½ pound joint of well-hung beef
    on the bone, for roasting
½ tablespoon all-purpose flour
generous ¾ cup strong beef stock
generous ¾ cup red wine
salt and pepper

to serve

popovers, see page 106
roasted potatoes, see page 100
glazed carrots
steamed broccoli
horseradish sauce (optional)
mustard (optional)

method

1 Preheat the oven to 425°F.

2 Rub a generous amount of olive oil and salt and pepper into the beef, then place in a roasting pan. Transfer to the preheated oven and roast for 30 minutes.

3 Reduce the temperature to 325°F and roast for an additional 60 minutes. Remove the beef from the ov Cover the beef with foil and let rest for at least 30 minutes.

4 Meanwhile, make the gravy. Remove the beef from the pan and stir the flour into the leftover juices. Ad the stock and wine, then simmer over a medium he until reduced by about half. Strain into a jug.

5 Cut the bones off the meat and carve the beef. Serv with the gravy, popovers, roasted potatoes, carrots, broccoli, and horseradish sauce and mustard, if liked

poached salmon

ingredients

serves 6

1 whole salmon, about 6 to 8
    pounds prepared weight
3 tablespoons salt
3 bay leaves
10 black peppercorns
1 onion, peeled and sliced
1 lemon, sliced
lemon wedges, to serve

method

1 Wipe the salmon thoroughly inside and out with pape
    towels, then use the back of a chef's knife to remove
    any scales that might still be on the skin. Remove the
    fins with a pair of scissors and trim the tail.

2 Place the salmon on the two-handled rack that come
    with a fish poacher, then place it in the poacher. Fill t
    poacher with enough cold water to cover the salmon
    adequately. Sprinkle over the salt, bay leaves, and
    peppercorns and scatter in the onion and lemon slic

3 Place the poacher over a low heat, over two burners
    and bring just to a boil, very slowly.

4 Cover and simmer very gently for 6–8 minutes. Let
    stand in the hot water for 15 minutes, then remove
    the fish carefully. Serve with lemon wedges for
    squeezing over.

variation

To serve cold, simmer for 2 minutes only, remove from
the heat, and let cool in the water for about 2 hours w
the lid on. Remove the skin when cool and decorate v
slices of cucumber.

something on the side

roasted root vegetables

ingredients

serves 4–6

3 parsnips, cut into 2-inch chunks

4 baby turnips, cut into quarters

3 carrots, cut into 2-inch chunks

1 pound butternut squash, peeled and cut into 2-inch chunks

1 pound sweet potatoes, peeled and cut into 2-inch chunks

2 garlic cloves, finely chopped

2 tablespoons chopped fresh rosemary

2 tablespoons chopped fresh thyme

2 teaspoons chopped fresh sage

3 tablespoons olive oil

salt and pepper

2 tablespoons chopped fresh mixed herbs, such as parsley, thyme, and mint, to garnish

method

1 Preheat the oven to 425°F.

2 Arrange all the vegetables in a single layer in a large roasting pan. Scatter over the garlic and the herbs. Po over the oil, and season well with salt and pepper.

3 Toss all the ingredients together until they are well mixed and coated with the oil. (You can leave them to marinate at this stage to allow the flavors to be absorbed.)

4 Roast the vegetables at the top of the preheated oven for 50–60 minutes, until they are cooked and nicely browned. Turn the vegetables over halfway through the cooking time.

5 Serve with a good handful of fresh herbs scattered o top and a final sprinkling of salt and pepper to taste.

sweet & sour red cabbage

ingredients

serves 6–8

1 red cabbage, about 1½ pounds
2 tablespoons olive oil
2 onions, finely sliced
1 garlic clove, chopped
2 small baking apples, peeled,
    cored, and sliced
2 tablespoons dark brown sugar
½ teaspoon ground cinnamon
1 teaspoon crushed juniper berries
whole nutmeg, for grating
2 tablespoons red wine vinegar
grated rind and juice of 1 orange
2 tablespoons cranberry jelly
salt and pepper

method

1 Cut the cabbage into quarters, remove the center stalk and finely shred the leaves.

2 Heat the oil in a large saucepan over a medium heat and add the cabbage, onions, garlic, and apples. Stir in the sugar, cinnamon, and juniper berries, and grate a quarter of the nutmeg into the pan.

3 Pour over the vinegar and orange juice, and add the orange rind.

4 Stir well and season to taste with salt and pepper. The pan will be quite full, but the volume of the cabbage will reduce during cooking.

5 Cook over a medium heat, stirring occasionally, until the cabbage is just tender but still has "bite". This will take 10–15 minutes, depending on how finely the cabbage is sliced.

6 Stir in the cranberry jelly, then taste and adjust the seasoning, adding salt and pepper if necessary. Serve immediately.

zucchini fritters

ingredients

makes 20–30 fritters

¾ cup self-rising flour
2 eggs, beaten
4 tablespoons milk
1 large zucchini
2 tablespoons fresh thyme,
plus extra to garnish
1 tablespoon oil
salt and pepper

method

1 Preheat the oven to 275°F.

2 Sift the flour into a large bowl and make a well in the center. Add the eggs to the well and stir, using a wooden spoon, gradually drawing in the flour. Slowly add the milk to the mixture, beating constantly to for a thick batter.

3 Meanwhile, grate the zucchini over a sheet of paper towel placed in a bowl to absorb some of the juices.

4 Add the zucchini, thyme, and salt and pepper, to tas to the batter and mix thoroughly, for about a minute

5 Heat the oil in a large, heavy-bottom skillet. Taking a tablespoon of the batter for a medium-sized fritter, half tablespoon of batter for a smaller-sized fritter, spoon the mixture into the hot oil and cook, in batc for 3–4 minutes on each side.

6 Remove the fritters with a slotted spoon and drain thoroughly on absorbent paper towels. Keep each batch warm in the oven while making the rest. Transfer to serving plates, garnish with the thyme, and serve immediately.

brussels sprouts with chestnuts

ingredients

serves 4

¾ pound brussels sprouts, trimmed
3 tablespoons butter
3½ ounces canned whole chestnuts
pinch of grated nutmeg
salt and pepper
½ cup slivered almonds, to garnish

method

1 Bring a large saucepan of lightly salted water to a boil Add the sprouts, bring back to a boil and cook for 5 minutes. Drain thoroughly.

2 Melt the butter in a large saucepan over a medium heat. Add the sprouts and cook, stirring, for 3 minute then add the chestnuts and nutmeg to the pan.

3 Season to taste with salt and pepper and stir well. Cook for a further 2 minutes, stirring, then remove from the heat.

4 Transfer to a warmed serving dish, scatter over the almonds and serve.

asparagus with lemon butter sauce

ingredients

serves 4

1¾ pounds asparagus spears, trimmed
1 tablespoon olive oil
salt and pepper

lemon butter sauce

juice of ½ lemon
2 tablespoons water
1 stick butter, cut into cubes
pepper

method

1 Preheat the oven to 400°F.

2 Lay the asparagus spears in a single layer on a large baking sheet. Drizzle over the oil, season to taste with salt and pepper, and roast in the preheated oven for 10 minutes, or until just tender.

3 Meanwhile, make the lemon butter sauce. Pour the lemon juice into a saucepan and add the water. Heat for a minute or so, then slowly add the butter, cube by cube, stirring constantly until it has all been incorporated. Season to taste with pepper, and serve warm with the asparagus.

roasted potatoes

ingredients

serves 6

3 pounds large mealy potatoes,
such as russet or Yukon gold,
cut into even-sized chunks

3 tablespoons goose fat, duck fat,
or olive oil

salt

method

1 Preheat the oven to 425°F.

2 Bring a large saucepan of lightly salted water to a bo
add the potatoes, bring back to a boil, and cook for
5–7 minutes. The potatoes should still be firm. Remo
from the heat.

3 Meanwhile, add the fat to a roasting pan and place t
pan in the preheated oven.

4 Drain the potatoes well and return them to the
saucepan. Cover with the lid and firmly shake the pa
so that the surface of the potatoes is roughened to
help give a much crisper texture.

5 Remove the roasting pan from the oven and carefu
pour the potatoes into the hot fat. Baste them to m
sure they are all coated with the fat.

6 Roast at the top of the oven for 45–50 minutes unt
they are browned all over and thoroughly crisp. Tur
the potatoes and baste again only once during the
process or the crunchy edges will be destroyed.

7 Carefully transfer the potatoes from the roasting pa
into a warmed serving dish. Sprinkle with a little sa
and serve immediately.

mashed potatoes

ingredients

serves 4

2 pounds mealy potatoes, such as
russet or Yukon gold, cut into
even-sized chunks
4 tablespoons butter
3 tablespoons hot milk
salt and pepper

method

1 Bring a large saucepan of lightly salted water to a boil,
add the potatoes, bring back to a boil, and cook for
20–25 minutes until they are tender. Test with the point
of a knife; but make sure you test right to the middle to
avoid lumps.

2 Remove the pan from the heat and drain the potatoes.
Return the potatoes to the hot pan and mash with a
potato masher until smooth.

3 Add the butter and continue to mash until it is all
mixed in, then add the milk. (It is better hot because
the potatoes absorb it more quickly to produce a
creamier mash.)

4 Taste the potatoes and season with salt and pepper if
necessary. Serve immediately.

scalloped potatoes

ingredients

serves 8

2 tablespoons butter, plus extra for
    greasing
1 tablespoon all-purpose flour
1 cup heavy cream
2 cups milk
1 teaspoon salt
pinch of freshly grated nutmeg
pinch of freshly ground
    white pepper
4 fresh thyme sprigs
2 garlic cloves, finely chopped
4½ pounds baking potatoes,
    thinly sliced
1 cup shredded Gruyère cheese or
    white cheddar cheese
salt and pepper

method

1 Preheat the oven to 375°F. Grease a 15 x 10-inch
   ovenproof dish.

2 Melt the butter in a saucepan over a medium heat. St
   in the flour and cook, stirring constantly, for 2 minute
   Gradually whisk in the cream and milk, and bring to
   simmering point. Add the salt, the nutmeg, white
   pepper, thyme, and garlic, reduce the heat to low, an
   simmer for 5 minutes. Remove the thyme sprigs.

3 Make a layer of half the potatoes in the prepared
   dish and season generously with salt and pepper. To
   with half the sauce and cover with half the cheese.
   Repeat the layers with the remaining potatoes, sauc
   and cheese.

4 Bake in the preheated oven for about 1 hour, or unti
   the top is browned and the potatoes are tender.
   Remove from the oven and let rest for 15 minutes
   before serving.

popovers

ingredients

makes 6 popovers

2 tablespoons beef fat or
　　sunflower oil
1 cup all-purpose flour
½ teaspoon salt
2 eggs
1 cup milk

method

1 Grease six metal popover molds with the fat or oil, then divide the remaining fat or oil between the molds. Preheat the oven to 425°F, placing the molds in the oven so the fat or oil can warm while the oven heats.

2 Sift the flour and salt together into a large mixing bowl and make a well in the center. Break the eggs into the well, add the milk and beat, gradually drawing in the flour from the side to make a smooth batter. Remove the molds from the oven and spoon in the batter until they are about half full.

3 Bake in the preheated oven for 30–35 minutes, without opening the oven door, until the popovers are well risen, puffed, and golden brown. Serve immediately, as they will collapse if left to stand.

hush puppies

ingredients
makes 30–35

2 cups yellow cornmeal
½ cup all-purpose flour, sifted
1 small onion, finely chopped
1 tablespoon superfine sugar
2 teaspoons baking powder
½ teaspoon salt
¾ cup milk
1 egg, beaten
corn oil, for deep-frying

method

1 Stir the cornmeal, flour, onion, sugar, baking powder, and salt together in a bowl, and make a well in the center.

2 Beat the milk and egg together in a jug, then pour into the dry ingredients and stir until a thick batter forms.

3 Heat at least 2 inches of oil in a deep skillet or saucepan over a high heat, until the temperature reaches 350°F, or until a cube of bread browns in 30 seconds.

4 Drop in as many teaspoonfuls of the batter as will fit without overcrowding the skillet, and cook, stirring constantly, until the hush puppies puff up and turn golden.

5 Remove from the oil with a slotted spoon and drain paper towels. Reheat the oil, if necessary, and cook th remaining batter. Serve hot.

gravy

ingredients

makes about 5 cups

2 pounds meat bones,
    raw or cooked
1 large onion, chopped
1 large carrot, chopped
2 celery stalks, chopped
1 bouquet garni
2 quarts water

method

1 Preheat the oven to 400°F. Put the bones in a roasting pan and roast in the preheated oven for 20 minutes, or until browned. Remove from the oven and leave to cool.

2 Chop the bones into small pieces and put in a large saucepan with all the remaining ingredients. Bring to a boil, then reduce the heat, cover and simmer for 2 hours.

3 Strain and leave until cold, then remove all traces of f Store, covered, in the refrigerator for up to 4 days. Bo vigorously for 5 minutes before using. The gravy can frozen in ice-cube trays for up to 1 month.

red wine sauce

ingredients

makes about 1 cup

⅔ cup gravy, (see page 110)
4 tablespoons red wine,
     such as a Burgundy
1 tablespoon red-currant jelly

method

1 Blend the gravy with the wine and pour into a small, heavy-bottom saucepan. Add the red-currant jelly and warm over a gentle heat, stirring, until blended.

2 Bring to a boil, then reduce the heat and simmer for 2 minutes. Serve hot.

coleslaw

ingredients

serves 10–12

⅔ cup mayonnaise
⅔ cup natural yogurt
dash of hot pepper sauce
1 head of white cabbage
4 carrots
1 green bell pepper, halved and
    seeded
salt and pepper

method

1 Mix the mayonnaise, yogurt, hot pepper sauce, and s
and pepper, to taste, together in a small bowl. Chill ir
the refrigerator until required.

2 Cut the cabbage in half and then into quarters. Rem
and discard the tough center stalk. Finely shred the
cabbage leaves. Wash the leaves under cold running
water and dry thoroughly on paper towels. Roughly
grate the carrots or shred in a food processor or on
mandoline. Finely chop the green bell pepper.

3 Mix the vegetables together in a large serving bow
and toss to mix. Pour over the dressing and toss un
the vegetables are well coated. Cover and chill in th
refrigerator until required.

corn relish

ingredients

makes about 2½ cups

5 corn cobs, about 2 pounds, husked
1 red bell pepper, seeded and finely diced
2 celery stalks, very finely chopped
1 red onion, finely chopped
½ cup plus 2 tablespoons sugar
1 tablespoon salt
2 tablespoons mustard powder
½ teaspoon celery seeds
small pinch of turmeric (optional)
1 cup apple cider vinegar
½ cup water

method

1 Bring a large saucepan of lightly salted water to a boil, and fill a bowl with icewater. Add the corn to the boiling water, return the water to a boil and boil for 2 minutes, or until the kernels are tender-crisp. Using tongs, immediately plunge the cobs into the cold water to halt cooking. Remove from the water and cut the kernels from the cobs, then set aside.

2 Add the red bell pepper, celery, and onion to the corn cooking water, bring back to a boil, and boil for 2 minutes, or until tender-crisp. Drain well and return to the pan with the corn kernels.

3 Put the sugar, salt, mustard, celery seeds, and turmeric if using, into a bowl and mix together. Then stir in the vinegar and water. Add to the pan, bring the liquid to a boil, then reduce the heat and simmer for 15 minutes, stirring occasionally.

4 Ladle the relish into hot, sterilized canning jars, filling them to within ½ inch of the top of each jar. Wipe the rims and secure the lids. Leave the relish to cool completely, then refrigerate for up to 2 months.

tomato sauce

ingredients

serves 4

1½ cups strained tomatoes
2 tablespoons chopped cilantro
1 tablespoon soy sauce
½ teaspoon chili powder
2 teaspoons dark brown sugar
2 teaspoons mild mustard
5 tablespoons vegetable stock

method

1 Combine all the ingredients in a small saucepan and bring to a boil. Reduce the heat to low, cover and simmer for 15 minutes.

2 Pour the mixture into a food processor or blender and blend well. Sieve thoroughly to remove any seeds.

3 Cool and serve immediately or store in the refrigerator until required.

classic strawberry jelly

ingredients
makes about 5 cups

3¼ pounds ripe, unblemished,
    whole strawberries, hulled
    and rinsed
2 freshly squeezed lemons,
    juice strained
7½ cups sugar
1 teaspoon butter

method

1 Place the strawberries in a large pan with the lemon juice, then simmer over a gentle heat for 15–20 minutes, stirring occasionally, until the fruit has collapsed and is very soft.

2 Add the sugar and heat, stirring occasionally, until sugar has completely dissolved. Add the butter, then bring to a boil and boil rapidly for 10–20 minutes, until the jelly has reached its setting point.

3 Leave to cool for 8–10 minutes, then skim and can warmed sterilized jars and immediately cover the with waxed discs. When completely cold, cover w cellophane or lids, label, and store in a cool place.

orange & squash marmalade

ingredients

makes about 7 cups

7 cups cubed acorn squash or
    butternut squash

6 blood oranges, scrubbed

⅔ cup freshly squeezed lemon
    juice

small piece fresh ginger, peeled
    and grated

2 serrano chiles, seeded and finely
    sliced

5 cups water

6¼ cups sugar

method

1 Place the squash in a large saucepan with a tight-fitting lid. Thinly slice two of the oranges without peeling, reserving the seeds, and add to the saucepan.

2 Peel the remaining oranges, chop the flesh and add to the pan together with the lemon juice, grated ginger, and sliced chiles. Tie up the orange seeds in a piece of muslin and add to the pan with the water.

3 Bring to a boil, then reduce the heat, cover and simmer gently for 1 hour, or until the squash and oranges are very soft.

4 Add the sugar and heat gently, stirring, until the sugar has completely dissolved. Bring to a boil and boil rapidly for 15 minutes, or until the setting point is reached.

5 Skim, if necessary, then leave to cool for 10 minutes. Can into warmed sterilized jars and immediately cover the tops with waxed discs. When completely cold, cover with cellophane or lids, label and store in a cool place.

cherry with brandy jam

ingredients

makes about 7 cups

4 pounds dark cherries, such as morello, rinsed and pitted

1 teaspoon freshly squeezed lemon juice or 1½ teaspoons citric or tartaric acid

⅔ cup water (optional)

2¾ pounds sugar

1 teaspoon butter

4 tablespoons brandy

1 cup liquid pectin

method

1 Roughly chop the cherries and place in a large pan with the lemon juice. If using citric or tartaric acid, add to the pan with the water. Place the pan over a gentle heat, cover and simmer gently for 20 minutes, or until the cherries have collapsed and are very soft.

2 Add the sugar and heat, stirring frequently, until the sugar has completely dissolved. Add the butter and brandy, bring to a boil and boil rapidly for 3 minutes. Remove from the heat and stir in the pectin.

3 Leave to cool for 10 minutes, then can into warmed sterilized jars and cover the tops with waxed discs. When completely cold, cover with cellophane or lids, label and store in a cool place.

variation

Other spirits or liqueurs can be used in place of the brandy. Try kirsch, an orange-flavored liqueur, or a whisky liqueur.

just desserts

apple pie

ingredients

serves 6

pie dough

2½ cups all-purpose flour, plus extra for dusting

pinch of salt

¾ stick butter or margarine, cut into small pieces

6 tablespoons lard or vegetable shortening, cut into small pieces

about 6 tablespoons cold water

beaten egg or milk, for glazing

filling

6–8 cups baking apples, peeled, cored and sliced

scant ⅔ cup light brown sugar or superfine sugar, plus extra for sprinkling

½–1 teaspoon ground cinnamon, mixed spice, or ground ginger

1–2 tablespoons water (optional)

method

1 To make the pie dough, sift the flour and salt into a mixing bowl. Add the butter and lard, and rub in with your fingertips until the mixture resembles fine breadcrumbs. Add the water and gather the mixture together into a dough. Wrap the dough and chill in the refrigerator for 30 minutes.

2 Preheat the oven to 425°F. Roll out almost two-thirds the dough thinly, and use to line a deep 9-inch pie plate or pie pan.

3 To make the filling, mix the apples with the sugar and spice, and pack into the pastry shell. Add the water if needed, particularly if the apples are not very juicy.

4 Roll out the remaining dough to form a lid. Dampen the edges of the pie rim with water and position the lid, pressing the edges firmly together. Trim and crimp the edges.

5 Using the dough trimmings, cut out leaves or other shapes to decorate the top of the pie. Dampen and attach. Glaze the top of the pie with the beaten egg and make one or two slits in the top.

6 Place the pie on a baking sheet and bake in the preheated oven for 20 minutes. Then reduce the oven temperature to 350°F and bake for an additional 30 minutes, or until the pastry is a light golden brown. Serve hot or cold, sprinkled with sugar.

bread & butter pudding

ingredients

serves 4–6

6 tablespoons butter, softened
6 thick slices of white bread
½ cup mixed dried fruit, such as
    currants and raisins
2 tablespoons candied citrus peel
3 extra-large eggs
1¼ cups milk
⅔ cup heavy cream
½ cup superfine sugar
whole nutmeg, for grating
1 tablespoon raw sugar
heavy cream, to serve (optional)

method

1 Preheat the oven to 350°F.

2 Use a little of the butter to grease an 8 x 10-inch baki
   dish. Butter the slices of bread, cut into quarters as
   triangles, and arrange half of the slices overlapping i
   the prepared baking dish.

3 Scatter half the fruit and candied peel over the brea
   cover with the remaining bread slices, then add the
   remaining fruit and candied peel.

4 In a pitcher, whisk the eggs well and mix in the milk
   cream, and sugar. Pour over the bread and let stand
   15 minutes to allow the bread to soak up some of th
   egg mixture. Tuck in most of the fruit since you don
   want it to burn in the oven.

5 Grate nutmeg, to taste, over the top of the pudding
   then sprinkle over the raw sugar.

6 Place the dish on a baking sheet and bake at the to
   the preheated oven for 30–40 minutes, until just se
   and golden brown.

7 Remove from the oven and serve warm with a little
   cream, if using.

banana cream pie

ingredients

serves 8–10

flour, for dusting
12 ounces prepared pastry dough,
    thawed, if frozen
4 extra-large egg yolks
heaping ¾ cup superfine sugar
4 tablespoons cornstarch
pinch of salt
2 cups milk
1 teaspoon vanilla extract
3 bananas
½ tablespoon lemon juice
1½ cups whipping cream,
    whipped with 3 tablespoons
    confectioners' sugar,
    to decorate

method

1 Preheat the oven to 400°F. Very lightly flour a rolling p
and use to roll out the dough on a lightly floured wor
surface into a 12-inch circle. Line a 9-inch pie plate wi
the dough, then trim the excess dough and pierce th
base all over with a fork. Line the pastry shell with
parchment paper and fill with baking beans.

2 Bake in the preheated oven for 15 minutes, or until th
pastry is a light golden color. Remove the paper and
beans and pierce the base again. Return to the oven
and bake for an additional 5–10 minutes, until golde
and dry. Leave to cool completely on a wire rack.

3 Meanwhile, put the egg yolks, sugar, cornstarch, and
salt into a bowl and beat until blended and pale in
color. Beat in the milk and vanilla extract.

4 Pour the mixture into a heavy-based saucepan over
medium–high heat and bring to a boil, stirring, unti
smooth and thick. Reduce the heat to low and simm
stirring, for 2 minutes. Strain the mixture into a bow
and set aside to cool.

5 Slice the bananas, place in a bowl with the lemon j
and toss. Arrange them in the cooled pastry shell, t
top with the custard and chill in the refrigerator for
least 2 hours. Spread the cream over the top of the
and serve immediately.

lemon meringue pie

ingredients

serves 6–8

pie dough

heaping 1 cup all-purpose flour,
    plus extra for dusting
¾ stick butter, cut into small
    pieces, plus extra for greasing
¼ cup superfine sugar, sifted
finely grated rind of
    ½ lemon
½ egg yolk, beaten
1½ tablespoons milk

filling

3 tablespoons cornflour
1¼ cups water
juice and grated rind of 2 lemons
heaping ¾ cup superfine sugar
2 eggs, separated

method

1 To make the pie dough, sift the flour into a bowl. Rub
the butter with your fingertips until the mixture
resembles fine breadcrumbs. Mix in the remaining
ingredients. Place the dough on a lightly floured work
surface and knead briefly. Wrap in plastic wrap and ch
in the refrigerator for 30 minutes.

2 Preheat the oven to 350°F. Grease an 8-inch round pie
pan. Roll out the pie dough to a thickness of ¼ inch,
then use it to line the base and side of the pan. Pierce
all over with a fork, line with parchment paper, and fi
with baking beans. Bake in the preheated oven for
15 minutes. Remove the pastry shell from the oven a
take out the paper and beans. Reduce the oven
temperature to 300°F.

3 To make the filling, mix the cornflour with a little of
the water to form a paste. Put the remaining water i
a saucepan. Stir in the lemon juice, lemon rind, and
cornflour paste. Bring to a boil, stirring, and cook for
2 minutes. Leave to cool slightly. Stir in 5 tablespoon
of the superfine sugar and the egg yolks, then pour
into the pastry shell.

4 Whisk the egg whites in a clean, grease-free bowl u
stiff. Gradually whisk in the remaining superfine sug
and spread over the pie. Bake for an additional
40 minutes. Remove from the oven, cool and serve

key lime pie

ingredients

serves 8

crumb crust

6 ounces graham crackers or
    ginger snaps
2 tablespoons granulated sugar
½ teaspoon ground cinnamon
5 tablespoons butter, melted,
    plus extra for greasing

filling

1¾ cups canned sweetened
    condensed milk
½ cup freshly squeezed lime juice
finely grated rind of 3 limes
4 egg yolks
whipped cream, to serve

method

1 Preheat the oven to 325°F. Lightly grease a 9-inch round pie pan, about 1½ inches deep.

2 To make the crumb crust, put the graham crackers, sugar, and cinnamon in a food processor and process until fine crumbs form–do not overprocess to a powder. Add the melted butter and process again until moistened.

3 Pour the crumb mixture into the prepared pie pan and press over the base and up the side. Place the pie pan on a baking tray and bake in the preheated oven for 5 minutes.

4 Meanwhile, to make the filling, beat the condensed milk, lime juice, lime rind, and egg yolks together in a bowl until well blended.

5 Remove the pie pan from the oven, pour the filling in the crumb crust and spread out to the edges. Return the oven for an additional 15 minutes, or until the filling is set around the edges but still wobbly in the center.

6 Let cool completely on a wire rack, then cover and ch for at least 2 hours. Spread thickly with whipped crea and serve.

rhubarb crisp

ingredients

serves 6

2 pounds rhubarb
½ cup sugar
grated rind and juice of 1 orange
homemade custard
    (see page 164), to serve

crisp

scant 1¾ cups all-purpose flour or
    wholemeal flour
½ cup unsalted butter, diced and
    chilled
½ cup light brown sugar
1 teaspoon ground ginger

method

1 Preheat the oven to 375°F.

2 Cut the rhubarb into 1-inch lengths and place in a 3½-pint ovenproof dish with the sugar and the orange rind and juice.

3 To make the crisp topping, place the flour in a mixing bowl and rub in the butter until the mixture resembles coarse breadcrumbs. Stir in the sugar and the ginger.

4 Spread the crisp topping evenly over the fruit and press down lightly using a fork.

5 Place on a baking sheet and bake in the center of the preheated oven for 25–30 minutes, until the crisp is golden brown. Serve warm with homemade custard.

baked rice pudding

ingredients

serves 4–6

1 tablespoon melted unsalted
    butter
½ cup white rice
¼ cup superfine sugar
3½ cups milk
½ teaspoon vanilla extract
3 tablespoons unsalted butter,
    chilled and cut into pieces
whole nutmeg, for grating
cream, jelly, fresh fruit purée,
    stewed fruit, honey or ice
    cream, to serve (optional)

method

1 Preheat the oven to 300°F. Grease a 2½-pint baking dish (a gratin dish is good) with the melted butter, place the rice in the dish, and sprinkle with the sugar.

2 Heat the milk in a saucepan until almost boiling, then pour over the rice. Add the vanilla extract and stir well to dissolve the sugar.

3 Cut the butter into small pieces and scatter over the surface of the pudding.

4 Grate nutmeg, to taste, over the top. Place the dish on a baking sheet, and bake in the center of the preheated oven for 1½–2 hours until the pudding is well browned on the top. Stir after the first 30 minutes of cooking to disperse the rice. Serve hot, topped with cream, if using.

new york cheesecake

ingredients

serves 10

1 stick butter, plus extra for
    greasing
1½ cups graham crackers,
    finely crushed
1 tablespoon granulated sugar

filling

4 cups cream cheese
1¼ cups superfine sugar
2 tablespoons all-purpose flour
1 teaspoon vanilla extract
finely grated zest of 1 orange
finely grated zest of 1 lemon
3 eggs
2 egg yolks
1½ cups heavy cream

method

1 Preheat the oven to 350°F. Place a small saucepan over
   low heat, add the butter and warm until it melts.
   Remove from the heat, stir in the graham crackers and
   granulated sugar, and mix through.

2 Press the crumb mixture tightly into the base of a
   9-inch springform cake pan. Place in the preheated
   oven and bake for 10 minutes. Remove from the oven
   and let cool on a wire rack.

3 Increase the oven temperature to 400°F. Use an elect
   mixer to beat the cheese until creamy, then gradually
   add the superfine sugar and flour and beat until
   smooth. Increase the speed and beat in the vanilla
   extract, orange zest, and lemon zest, then beat in
   the eggs and egg yolks one at a time. Finally, beat in
   the cream.

4 Grease the side of the cake pan and pour in the
   filling. Smooth the top, transfer to the oven, and bak
   for 15 minutes, then reduce the temperature to 225
   and bake for an additional 30 minutes. Turn off the
   oven and leave the cheesecake in it for 2 hours to c
   and set. Cover and chill in the refrigerator overnigh

5 Slide a knife around the edge of the cake, then
   unfasten the pan. Cut the cheesecake into slices
   and serve.

caramel-topped date pudding

ingredients

serves 4

heaping ½ cup golden raisins
1 cup pitted chopped dates
1 teaspoon baking soda
2 tablespoons butter, plus extra
    for greasing
1 cup light brown sugar
2 eggs
1⅓ cups self-rising flour, sifted

caramel sauce

2 tablespoons butter
scant ¾ cup heavy cream
1 cup light brown sugar
zested rind of 1 orange, to decorate
freshly whipped cream, to serve
    (optional)

method

1 To make the base, put the golden raisins, dates, and baking soda into an ovenproof bowl. Cover with boiling water and leave to soak.

2 Preheat the oven to 350°F. Grease an 8-inch round cake pan.

3 Put the butter in a separate bowl, add the sugar and mix well. Beat in the eggs then fold in the flour. Drain the soaked fruit, add to the bowl and mix. Spoon the mixture evenly into the prepared cake pan.

4 Transfer to the preheated oven and bake for 35–40 minutes. The pudding is cooked when a skewer inserted into the center comes out clean.

5 About 5 minutes before the end of the cooking time, make the sauce. Melt the butter in a saucepan over a medium heat. Stir in the cream and sugar and bring to a boil, stirring constantly. Reduce the heat and simmer for 5 minutes.

6 Place the pudding onto a serving plate and pour over the sauce. Decorate with zested orange rind and serve with whipped cream, if using.

chocolate pudding

ingredients

serves 4–6

½ cup sugar

4 tablespoons unsweetened
    cocoa powder

2 tablespoons cornstarch

pinch of salt

1½ cups milk

1 egg, beaten

4 tablespoons butter

½ teaspoon vanilla extract

heavy cream, to serve

method

1 Put the sugar, cocoa powder, cornstarch, and salt into an ovenproof bowl, stir and set aside.

2 Pour the milk into a saucepan and heat over medium heat until just simmering. Do not bring to a boil.

3 Keeping the pan over a medium heat, spoon a little of the simmering milk into the sugar mixture and blend, then stir this mixture into the milk in the pan. Beat in the egg and half the butter, and reduce the heat to low.

4 Simmer for 5–8 minutes, stirring frequently, until the mixture thickens. Remove from the heat, add the vanilla extract and the remaining butter, stirring until the butter melts and is absorbed.

5 The pudding can be served hot or chilled, with cream for pouring over it. If chilling the pudding, spoon it into a serving bowl and leave to cool completely. Then press plastic wrap onto the surface to prevent a skin from forming and chill in the refrigerator until required.

pecan pie

ingredients

serves 8

pie dough

1¾ cups all-purpose flour,
   plus extra for dusting
1 stick unsalted butter, cut into
   small pieces
2 tablespoons superfine sugar
a little cold water

filling

5 tablespoons unsalted butter
scant ½ cup light brown sugar
⅔ cup light corn syrup
2 extra-large eggs, beaten
1 teaspoon vanilla extract
1 cup pecans

method

1 To make the pie dough, place the flour in a bowl
   and rub in the butter with your fingertips until it
   resembles fine breadcrumbs. Stir in the sugar and add
   enough cold water to the mix to a firm dough. Wrap in
   plastic wrap and chill for 15 minutes, until firm enough
   to roll out.

2 Preheat the oven to 400°F. Roll out the dough on a
   lightly floured surface and use it to line a 9-inch
   loose-bottom round pie pan. Pierce the base with a
   fork. Chill for 15 minutes.

3 Place the pie pan on a baking tray and line with a she
   of parchment paper and baking beans. Bake in the
   preheated oven for 10 minutes. Remove the baking
   beans and paper, and bake for an additional 5 minute
   Reduce the oven temperature to 350°F.

4 To make the filling, place the butter, sugar, and light
   corn syrup in a saucepan and heat gently until melte
   Remove from the heat and quickly beat in the eggs
   and vanilla extract.

5 Roughly chop the nuts and stir into the mixture. Pou
   into the pastry shell and bake for 35–40 minutes, un
   the filling is just set. Serve warm or cold.

pumpkin pie

ingredients

serves 6

4 pounds pumpkin, halved and
    seeded
1 cup all-purpose flour, plus extra
    for dusting
¼ teaspoon baking powder
1½ teaspoons ground cinnamon
¾ teaspoon ground nutmeg
¾ teaspoon ground cloves
1 teaspoon salt
½ cup superfine sugar
4 tablespoons unsalted butter,
    chilled and diced, plus extra for
    greasing
3 eggs
1¾ cups canned sweetened
    condensed milk
½ teaspoon vanilla extract
1 tablespoon raw brown sugar

streusel topping

2 tablespoons all-purpose flour
4 tablespoons raw brown sugar
1 teaspoon ground cinnamon
2 tablespoons unsalted butter,
    chilled and diced
heaping ⅔ cup pecan nuts,
    chopped
heaping ⅔ cup walnuts, chopped

method

1 Preheat the oven to 375°F. Bake the pumpkin halves,
    face down in a shallow pan, covered with foil, for
    1½ hours. When cool, puree the flesh in a food
    processor. Drain off any liquid, cover, and chill.

2 Grease a 9-inch round pie pan. Sift the flour and
    baking powder into a bowl. Stir in ½ teaspoon of the
    cinnamon, ¼ teaspoon of the nutmeg, ¼ teaspoon of
    the cloves, ½ teaspoon of the salt, and all the superfin
    sugar. Rub in the butter until the mixture resembles
    fine breadcrumbs, then make a well in the center.
    Lightly beat 1 of the eggs and pour it into the well. M
    together, then shape into a ball. Roll out the dough o
    a lightly floured work surface and line the pan. Trim th
    edges, cover and chill for 30 minutes.

3 Preheat the oven to 425°F. Put the pumpkin puree in
    large bowl, then stir in the condensed milk, the
    remaining eggs, spices, salt, vanilla extract, and raw
    brown sugar. Pour into the pastry shell and bake in t
    preheated oven for 15 minutes.

4 For the streusel topping, mix the flour, sugar, and
    cinnamon together in a bowl. Rub in the butter, the
    stir in the nuts. Reduce the oven temperature to 35(
    Sprinkle the topping over the pie then return to the
    oven and bake for an additional 35 minutes.
    Serve warm.

latticed cherry pie

ingredients

serves 8

pie dough

heaping 1 cup all-purpose flour,
    plus extra for dusting
¼ teaspoon baking powder
½ teaspoon mixed spice
½ teaspoon salt
¼ cup superfine sugar
½ stick butter, chilled and diced,
    plus extra for greasing
1 egg, beaten, plus extra for
    glazing
water, for sealing

filling

5¾ cups (about 2 pounds) pitted
    fresh cherries,
    or canned cherries, drained
¾ cup superfine sugar
½ teaspoon almond extract
2 teaspoons cherry brandy
¼ teaspoon mixed spice
2 tablespoons cornstarch
2 tablespoons water
2 tablespoons unsalted butter,
    melted

method

1 To make the pie dough, sift the flour with the baking powder into a large bowl. Stir in the mixed spice, salt, and sugar. Rub in the butter until the mixture resemble fine breadcrumbs. Make a well in the center, pour in th egg, and mix into a dough. Cut the dough in half, wra and chill for 30 minutes.

2 Preheat the oven to 425°F. Grease a 9-inch round pie dish. Roll out the dough into two rounds, each 12 inches in diameter. Use one to line the pie dish.

3 To make the filling, put half the cherries and all the sugar in a saucepan. Bring to a simmer and stir in the almond extract, brandy, and mixed spice. In a bowl, m the cornstarch and water into a paste. Stir the paste into the saucepan, then boil until the mixture thicker Stir in the remaining cherries, pour into the pastry sh then drizzle with the melted butter.

4 Cut the remaining pastry into strips ½ inch wide. Lay the strips over the filling, crossing to form a lattice. T and seal the edges with water. Use your fingers to crimp the rim, then glaze the top with the beaten e Cover with foil, then bake for 30 minutes in the preheated oven. Discard the foil, then bake for an additional 15 minutes, or until golden. Serve warm.

indian pudding

ingredients
serves 4–6

2 tablespoons raisins
5 tablespoons coarse yellow
    cornmeal
1½ cups milk
4 tablespoons dark molasses
2 tablespoons raw brown sugar
½ teaspoon salt
2 tablespoons butter, diced,
    plus extra for greasing
2 teaspoons ground ginger
¼ teaspoon cinnamon
¼ teaspoon ground nutmeg
2 eggs, beaten
vanilla ice cream or maple syrup,
    to serve

method

1 Preheat the oven to 300°F. Generously grease a 4-cup ovenproof serving dish and set aside. Put the raisins in a sieve with 1 tablespoon of the cornmeal and toss well together. Shake off the excess cornmeal and set aside.

2 Put the milk and molasses into a saucepan over a medium–high heat and stir until the molasses is dissolved. Add the sugar and salt and continue stirring until the sugar is dissolved. Sprinkle over the remaining cornmeal and bring to a boil, stirring constantly. Reduce the heat and simmer for 3–5 minutes, until the mixture is thickened.

3 Remove the pan from the heat, add the butter, ginger, cinnamon, and nutmeg, and stir until the butter is melted. Add the eggs and beat until they are incorporated, then stir in the raisins. Pour the mixture into the prepared dish.

4 Put the dish in a small roasting pan, and pour in enough boiling water to come halfway up the side of the dish. Put the dish in the preheated oven and bake, uncovered, for 1¾–2 hours, until the pudding is set and a toothpick inserted in the center comes out clean.

5 Serve immediately, straight from the dish, with a dollop of ice cream on top.

apple turnovers

ingredients
makes 8 turnovers

9 ounces prepared puff pastry,
    thawed, if frozen
flour, for dusting
milk, for glazing

filling
1 pound cooking apples, peeled,
    cored, and chopped
grated rind of 1 lemon (optional)
pinch of ground cloves (optional)
3 tablespoons sugar

orange sugar
1 tablespoon sugar, for sprinkling
finely grated rind of 1 orange

orange cream
1 cup heavy cream
grated rind of 1 orange and juice of
    ½ orange
confectioners' sugar, to taste

method

1 To make the filling, mix together the apples, lemon rind, and ground cloves, if using, but do not add the sugar. For the orange sugar, mix together the sugar and orange rind.

2 Preheat the oven to 425°F. Roll out the pastry on a floured work surface into a 24 x 12-inch rectangle. Cut the pastry in half lengthwise, then across into four to make eight 6-inch squares.

3 Mix the sugar into the apple filling. Brush each square lightly with milk and place a little of the apple filling in the center. Fold one corner over diagonally to meet the opposite one, making a triangular turnover, and press the edges together very firmly. Place on a nonstick baking sheet. Repeat with the remaining squares.

4 Brush the turnovers with milk and sprinkle with a little of the orange sugar. Bake for 15–20 minutes, until puffed and well browned. Cool the turnovers on a wire rack.

5 For the orange cream, whip the cream, orange rind, and orange juice together until thick. Add a little sugar to taste and whip again. Serve the turnovers warm, with dollops of orange cream.

apple fritters

ingredients
makes 12 fritters

2¼ cups (about 3 medium) eating
    apples, such as Granny Smith,
    peeled, cored, and diced
1 teaspoon lemon juice
2 eggs, separated
sunflower oil, for deep-frying
    and for greasing
⅔ cup milk
1 tablespoon butter, melted
½ cup all-purpose flour
½ cup whole wheat flour
2 tablespoons sugar
¼ teaspoon salt

cinnamon glaze
½ cup confectioners' sugar
½ teaspoon ground cinnamon
1 tablespoon milk, plus extra, if
    needed

method

1 To make the cinnamon glaze, sift the sugar and
cinnamon into a small bowl. Slowly stir in the milk unt
smooth, then set aside.

2 Put the apples in a small bowl, add the lemon juice,
toss and set aside. Beat the egg whites in a separate
bowl until stiff peaks form, then set aside.

3 Heat enough oil for deep-frying in a deep-fat fryer or
heavy-bottom saucepan until it reaches 350°F, or unt
a cube of bread browns in 30 seconds.

4 Put the egg yolks and milk into a large bowl and bea
together, then stir in the butter. Sift both the flours, t
sugar and salt together, then stir the dry ingredients
into the wet ingredients until just combined. Stir in
apples and their juices, then fold in the egg whites.

5 Lightly grease a spoon and use it to drop batter into
the hot oil, without overcrowding the pan. Fry the
fritters for 2–3 minutes, turning once, until golden
brown on both sides. Drain on paper towels, then
transfer to a wire rack. Repeat until all the batter is u

6 Stir the glaze and add a little extra milk, if necessary
Drizzle the glaze over the fritters and let stand for
3–5 minutes to firm up. Serve immediately.

banana splits

ingredients

serves 4

4 bananas
6 tablespoons chopped mixed
    nuts, to serve

vanilla ice cream

1¼ cups milk
1 teaspoon vanilla extract
3 egg yolks
½ cup superfine sugar
1¼ cups heavy cream, whipped

chocolate sauce

4½ ounces dark chocolate,
    broken into small pieces
2½ tablespoons butter
6 tablespoons water
1 tablespoon rum

method

1 To make the vanilla ice cream, heat the milk and vanilla extract in a saucepan over a medium heat until almost boiling. Beat the egg yolks and sugar together in a bowl. Remove the milk from the heat and stir a little into the egg mixture. Transfer the mixture back to the pan, and stir over a low heat until thickened. Do not allow to boil. Remove from the heat.

2 Let cool for about 30 minutes, fold in the cream, cover with plastic wrap, and chill in the refrigerator for 1 hour. Transfer to an ice-cream maker and process for 15 minutes.

3 Alternatively, transfer into a freezerproof container and freeze for 1 hour, then place in a bowl and beat to break up the ice crystals. Return to the container and freeze for 30 minutes. Repeat twice more, freezing for 30 minutes and whisking each time.

4 To make the chocolate sauce, melt the chocolate and butter with the water in a saucepan, stirring constantly. Remove from the heat and stir in the rum. Peel the bananas, slice lengthwise, and arrange on four serving dishes. Top with ice cream and nuts and serve with the sauce.

chocolate fudge

ingredients

makes 32 pieces

2 tablespoons unsweetened cocoa
    powder

1¼ cups milk

4½ ounces bittersweet chocolate,
    at least 85 percent cocoa solids,
    finely chopped

4 cups superfine sugar

½ cup butter, chopped, plus extra
    for greasing

pinch of salt

1½ teaspoons vanilla extract

1½ cups chopped pecan nuts,
    walnuts, or toasted hazelnuts,
    or a mixture of nuts

method

1 Line an 8-inch square cake pan with greased foil.

2 Put the cocoa powder into a small bowl, add
    2 tablespoons of the milk and stir until blended. Pour
    the remaining milk into a large, heavy-bottom
    saucepan, then add the cocoa mixture and chocolate
    and simmer over a medium–high heat, stirring, until
    the chocolate melts. Add the sugar, butter, and salt.
    Reduce the heat to low and stir until the butter is
    melted, the sugar is dissolved, and you can't feel any
    the grains when you rub a spoon against the side of
    the pan.

3 Increase the heat and bring the mixture to a boil.
    Cover the pan and boil for 2 minutes, then uncover
    and continue boiling, without stirring, until the
    temperature reaches 240°F, or until a small amount
    of the mixture forms a soft ball when dropped in
    cold water.

4 Remove the pan from the heat, stir in the vanilla
    extract, and beat the fudge until it thickens. Stir in th
    nuts. Pour the fudge mixture into the prepared pan
    and use a wet spatula to smooth the surface. Set as
    and leave to stand for at least 2 hours to become fir
    Lift the fudge out of the pan, then peel off the foil a
    cut into squares. Store the fudge for up to one wee
    an airtight container.

homemade custard

ingredients

serves 4–6

1¼ cups milk
2 eggs
2 teaspoons superfine sugar
1 vanilla bean, split,
    or 1 teaspoon vanilla extract

method

1 Put 2 tablespoons of the milk, the eggs, and the sugar into an ovenproof bowl that will fit over a saucepan of simmering water without the bottom of the bowl touching the water, then set aside.

2 Heat the remaining milk just until small bubbles appear around the edge. Scrape half the vanilla seeds into the milk and add the bean. Remove the pan from the heat, cover and leave to infuse for 30 minutes.

3 Bring a kettle of water to a boil. Meanwhile, using an electric mixer, beat the milk, eggs, and sugar until pale and thick. Slowly beat in the warm milk.

4 Pour a thin layer of boiling water into a saucepan, place over a low heat and place the bowl containing the milk mixture on top. Cook, stirring constantly, for 10–15 minutes, until the sauce thickens. It is important that the bottom of the bowl never touches the water and that the sauce doesn't boil.

5 Strain the hot custard into a pitcher. Stir in the vanilla extract (if using). The custard can be used immediately or cooled and chilled for up to one day. It will thicken upon cooling.

chocolate brandy sauce

ingredients

serves 4

9 ounces semisweet chocolate
    (must contain at least
    50 percent cocoa solids)
½ cup heavy cream
2 tablespoons brandy

method

1 Break or chop the chocolate into small pieces, and place in the top of a double boiler or in an ovenproof bowl set over a saucepan of simmering water.

2 Pour in the cream and stir until melted and smooth. Stir in the brandy, pour into a pitcher, and serve.

white chocolate fudge sauce

ingredients

serves 4

⅔ cup heavy cream

4 tablespoons unsalted butter, cut into small pieces

3 tablespoons superfine sugar

6 ounces white chocolate, broken into pieces

2 tablespoons brandy

method

1 Pour the cream into the top of a double boiler or an ovenproof bowl set over a saucepan of gently simmering water. Add the butter and sugar, and stir until the mixture is smooth. Remove from the heat.

2 Stir in the chocolate, a few pieces at a time, waiting until each batch has melted before adding the next. Add the brandy and stir the sauce until smooth. Cool to room temperature before serving.

variation

Give this sauce a citrus zing by replacing the brandy with the same quantity of an orange-flavored liqueur.

baked delights

classic oatmeal cookies

ingredients

makes 30 cookies

¾ cup butter, plus extra for
    greasing
scant 1⅓ cups raw brown sugar
1 egg
4 tablespoons water
1 teaspoon vanilla extract
4½ cups rolled oats
1 cup all-purpose flour
1 teaspoon salt
½ teaspoon baking soda

method

1 Preheat the oven to 350°F and grease a large cookie sheet.

2 Cream the butter and sugar together in a large mixing bowl. Beat in the egg, water, and vanilla extract until the mixture is smooth. In a separate bowl, mix the oat flour, salt, and baking soda.

3 Gradually stir the oat mixture into the creamed mixture until thoroughly combined.

4 Place tablespoonfuls of the mixture onto the prepared cookie sheet, making sure they are well spaced. Transfer to the preheated oven and bake for 15 minutes, or until the cookies are golden brown.

5 Using a palette knife, carefully transfer the cookies to wire racks to cool completely.

black & white cookies

ingredients

makes 20 cookies

½ cup unsalted butter, plus extra
　for greasing
1 teaspoon vanilla extract
1¾ cups superfine sugar
2 eggs, beaten
2½ cups all-purpose flour
½ teaspoon baking powder
¾ cup milk

icing

1¾ cups confectioners' sugar
½ cup heavy cream
⅛ teaspoon vanilla extract
2¾ ounces semisweet chocolate,
　broken into pieces

method

1 Preheat the oven to 375°F. Grease three cookie sheets. Place the butter, vanilla extract, and sugar in a large bowl. Beat the mixture with a whisk until light and fluffy, and then beat in the eggs one at a time.

2 Sift the flour and baking powder and fold into the creamed mixture, loosening with milk as you go until both are used up and the mixture is of dropping consistency.

3 Drop heaped tablespoonfuls of the mixture, spaced well apart, on the prepared cookie sheets. Place in the preheated oven and bake for 15 minutes until turning golden at the edges and light to the touch. Transfer to wire racks to cool completely.

4 To make the icing, put the sugar in a bowl and mix in half the cream and all the vanilla extract. The consistency should be thick but spreadable. Using a small palette knife, spread half of each cookie with white icing. Now, melt the chocolate in an ovenproof bowl over a pan of simmering water. The base of the bowl should not touch the water. Remove from the heat and stir in the remaining cream. Spread the dark icing over the uncoated cookie halves.

chocolate chip cookies

ingredients

makes 30 cookies

1¼ cups all-purpose flour
1 teaspoon baking powder
generous ½ cup margarine,
   plus extra for greasing
⅓ cup light brown sugar
¼ cup superfine sugar
½ teaspoon vanilla extract
1 egg
4½ ounces semisweet chocolate
   chips

method

1 Preheat the oven to 375°F. Lightly grease two cookie sheets.

2 Place all of the ingredients in a large mixing bowl and beat until well combined.

3 Place tablespoonfuls of the mixture on the prepared cookie sheets, spacing them well apart to allow for spreading during cooking.

4 Bake in the preheated oven for 10–12 minutes, or until the cookies are golden brown. Using a palette knife, transfer the cookies to a wire rack to cool completely.

5 Serve immediately or store in an airtight container.

chocolate caramel shortbread

ingredients
makes 12 slices

1 stick butter, plus extra for
  greasing
heaping 1 cup all-purpose flour
heaping ¼ cup granulated sugar
7 ounces semisweet chocolate,
  broken into pieces

filling
1½ sticks butter
heaping ½ cup superfine sugar
3 tablespoons light corn syrup
1 (14-fluid ounce) can sweetened
  condensed milk

method

1 Preheat the oven to 350°F. Grease and line the base of
  9-inch shallow, square cake pan.

2 Place the butter, flour, and sugar in a food processor
  and process until the mixture begins to bind togethe
  Press it into the prepared pan and smooth the top.
  Bake in the preheated oven for 20–25 minutes,
  or until golden.

3 Meanwhile, make the filling. Place the butter,
  sugar, light corn syrup, and condensed milk in a
  saucepan and heat gently over a low heat until the
  sugar is dissolved.

4 Bring to a boil and simmer for 6–8 minutes, stirring
  constantly, until the mixture becomes very thick. Po
  over the shortbread base and leave to chill in the
  refrigerator until firm.

5 Place the chocolate in an ovenproof bowl set over a
  saucepan of gently simmering water and stir until
  melted. Let cool slightly, then spread over the caram
  Chill in the refrigerator until set. Cut the shortbread
  12 pieces with a sharp knife and serve.

chocolate brownies

ingredients

makes 16 squares

peanut oil, for greasing
8 ounces semisweet chocolate,
    at least 60 percent cocoa solids
¾ cup butter
3 extra-large eggs
½ cup superfine sugar
scant 1¼ cups self-rising flour
1 cup walnuts or blanched
    hazelnuts, chopped
scant ⅓ cup milk chocolate chips

method

1 Preheat the oven to 350°F. Lightly grease a 10-inch square nonstick, shallow baking pan.

2 Break the chocolate into an ovenproof bowl and place over a small saucepan of simmering water. It is important that the base of the bowl doesn't touch the water.

3 Add the butter to the chocolate, keeping the bowl over the saucepan and heating the water to a slow simmer. Leave the chocolate, undisturbed, to melt very slowly—this will take about 10 minutes. Remove the bowl from the pan and stir well to combine the chocolate and the butter.

4 Meanwhile, beat the eggs and sugar together in a bowl until pale cream in color. Stir in the melted chocolate mixture, then add the flour, nuts, and chocolate chips. Mix everything together well.

5 Pour the mixture into the prepared baking pan and bake in the preheated oven for 30 minutes, or until the top is set—if the center is still slightly sticky, that will even better. Leave to cool in the pan, then lift out and cut into squares.

bran muffins with raisins

ingredients
makes 12 muffins

1 cup all-purpose flour
1 tablespoon baking powder
2¼ cups wheat bran
heaping ½ cup superfine sugar
1 cup raisins
2 large eggs
1 cup skim milk
6 tablespoons sunflower oil,
    plus extra for greasing
1 teaspoon vanilla extract

method

1 Preheat the oven to 400°F. Grease a 12-cup muffin pan or line with 12 paper cases. Sift the flour and baking powder together into a large bowl. Stir in the bran, sugar, and raisins.

2 Lightly beat the eggs in a large pitcher or bowl, then beat in the milk, oil, and vanilla extract. Make a well in the center of the dry ingredients and pour in the beaten liquid ingredients. Stir gently until just combined; do not overmix.

3 Spoon the mixture into the prepared muffin pan. Bake in the preheated oven for about 20 minutes, until well risen, golden brown, and firm to the touch.

4 Leave the muffins in the pan for 5 minutes, then serve warm or transfer to a wire rack and let cool complete

vanilla-frosted cupcakes

ingredients
makes 12 cupcakes

½ cup butter, softened
½ cup superfine sugar
2 eggs, lightly beaten
scant 1 cup self-rising flour
1 tablespoon milk
1 tablespoon colored sprinkles

frosting
¾ cup unsalted butter, softened
1 teaspoon vanilla extract
2¼ cups confectioners' sugar,
    sifted

method

1 Preheat the oven to 350°F. Put 12 paper baking cases in a muffin tray or 12 double-layer paper cases on a cookie sheet.

2 Put the butter and sugar in a bowl. Beat together until light and fluffy. Gradually beat in the eggs. Sift in the flour and fold in the milk.

3 Spoon the mixture into the paper cases. Bake in the preheated oven for 20 minutes until golden brown and firm to the touch. Transfer to a wire rack to cool.

4 To make the frosting, put the butter and vanilla extract in a bowl and beat until pale and very soft. Gradually add the sugar, beating well after each addition.

5 Spoon the frosting into a large piping bag equipped with a medium star-shaped tip, and pipe swirls of frosting on the top of each cupcake. Serve decorated with sprinkles.

scones

ingredients
makes 10–12 scones

3⅔ cups all-purpose flour,
  plus extra for dusting
½ teaspoon salt
2 teaspoons baking powder
4 tablespoons butter
2 tablespoons superfine sugar
1¼ cups milk
3 tablespoons milk, for glazing
classic strawberry jelly
  (see page 120) and clotted
  cream, to serve

method

1 Preheat the oven to 425°F. Lightly flour a baking sheet.

2 Sift the flour, salt, and baking powder into a bowl. Rub in the butter until the mixture resembles breadcrumbs. Stir in the sugar. Make a well in the center and pour in the milk. Stir in using a round-bladed knife and make a soft dough.

3 Place the dough onto a floured work surface and lightly flatten by hand until it is an even thickness, about ½ inch. Don't be too heavy-handed—scones need a light touch.

4 Use a 2½-inch cookie cutter to cut out the scone shapes, then place them on the prepared baking sheet. Glaze with a little milk and bake in the preheated oven for 10–12 minutes, until golden and well risen.

5 Let cool on a wire rack. Serve freshly baked, with strawberry jelly and clotted cream.

strawberry shortcakes

ingredients

serves 6

2 cups self-rising flour, plus extra
    for dusting
½ teaspoon baking powder
½ cup superfine sugar
¾ stick butter, plus extra for
    greasing
1 egg, beaten
2–3 tablespoons milk, plus extra
    for brushing

filling

1 teaspoon vanilla extract
heaping 1 cup mascarpone cheese
3 tablespoons confectioners' sugar,
    plus extra for dusting
3½ cups strawberries

method

1 Preheat the oven to 350°F. Lightly grease a large
    baking sheet.

2 Sift the flour, baking powder, and sugar together into
    bowl. Rub in the butter until the mixture resembles
    breadcrumbs. Beat the egg with 2 tablespoons of the
    milk. Stir into the dry ingredients with a fork to form a
    soft, but not sticky, dough, adding more milk if needed

3 Place the dough onto a lightly floured surface and rol
    out to about ¾ inch thick. Cut out rounds, using a
    2³/₄-inch cookie cutter. Lightly press the trimmings
    together and cut out more rounds.

4 Place on the baking sheet and brush the tops lightly
    with milk. Bake for 12–15 minutes, until firm and
    golden brown. Place on a wire rack to cool.

5 To make the filling, stir the vanilla extract into the
    cheese with 2 tablespoons of the sugar. Reserve a fev
    whole strawberries for decoration, then hull and slice
    the rest. Sprinkle with the remaining sugar.

6 Split the shortcakes in half horizontally. Spoon half th
    cheese mixture onto the bases and top with the slic
    strawberries. Spoon over the remaining cheese mixt
    and replace the tops. Dust the shortcakes with suga
    and top with the reserved whole strawberries.

cinnamon swirls

ingredients
makes 12 swirls

1⅔ cups white bread flour
½ teaspoon salt
2¼ teaspoons active dry yeast
2 tablespoons butter, cut into small pieces, plus extra for greasing
1 egg, lightly beaten
½ cup lukewarm milk
2 tablespoons maple syrup, for glazing

filling

4 tablespoons butter, softened
2 teaspoons ground cinnamon
¼ cup light brown sugar
⅓ cup currants

method

1 Grease a baking sheet with a little butter.

2 Sift the flour and salt into a mixing bowl. Stir in the yeast. Rub in the butter with your fingertips until the mixture resembles breadcrumbs. Add the egg and mi and mix to form a dough.

3 Form the dough into a ball, place in a greased bowl, cover and let stand in a warm place for about 40 minutes, or until doubled in size.

4 Lightly punch down the dough for 1 minute, then rol out to a rectangle measuring 12 x 9 inches.

5 To make the filling, cream together the butter, cinnamon, and sugar until light and fluffy. Spread the filling evenly over the dough rectangle, leaving a 1-inch border all around. Sprinkle the currants evenly over the top.

6 Roll up the dough from one of the long edges, and press down to seal. Cut the roll into 12 slices. Place them, cut-side down, on the baking sheet. Cover and let stand for 30 minutes.

7 Meanwhile, preheat the oven to 375°F. Bake the bun the preheated oven for 20–30 minutes, or until well risen. Brush with the maple syrup and let cool slight before serving.

apple cake

ingredients

serves 8

1 pound baking apples
1¼ cups self-rising flour
1 teaspoon ground cinnamon
pinch of salt
1 stick butter, plus extra for
    greasing
heaping ½ cup superfine sugar
2 eggs
1–2 tablespoons milk
confectioners' sugar, for dusting

topping

generous ¾ cup self-rising flour
¾ stick butter
scant ½ cup superfine sugar

method

1 Preheat the oven to 350°F, then grease a 9-inch springform cake pan. To make the topping, sift the flour into a bowl and rub in the butter until the mixture resembles coarse breadcrumbs. Stir in the sugar and reserve.

2 To make the cake, peel, core, and thinly slice the apples. Sift the flour into a bowl with the cinnamon and salt. Place the butter and sugar in a separate bowl and beat together until light and fluffy. Gradually beat in the eggs, adding a little of the flour mixture with the last addition of egg. Gently fold in half of the remaining flour mixture, then fold in the rest with the milk.

3 Spoon the batter into the prepared pan and smooth the top. Cover with the sliced apples and sprinkle over the topping evenly.

4 Bake in the preheated oven for 1 hour, or until browned and firm to the touch. Leave to cool in the pan before opening the sides. Dust the cake with the sugar before serving.

raspberry layer cake

ingredients

serves 8–10

¾ cup butter, at room temperature,
    plus extra for greasing
¾ cup superfine sugar
3 eggs, beaten
scant 1½ cups self-rising flour
pinch of salt
raspberry jelly
heavy cream, whipped
1 tablespoon confectioners' sugar
    or superfine sugar, for dusting

method

1 Preheat the oven to 350°F. Grease two 8-inch cake par
and line with wax paper or parchment paper.

2 Cream the butter and sugar together in a mixing bow
using a wooden spoon or a handheld mixer until the
batter is pale in color and light and fluffy. Add the eg(
a little at a time, beating well after each addition.

3 Sift the flour and salt together and carefully add to th
batter, folding in with a metal spoon. Divide the batte
between the pans and smooth over the surface.

4 Place the pans on the same shelf in the center of the
preheated oven and bake for 25–30 minutes until we
risen, golden brown, and beginning to shrink from th
sides of the pans.

5 Remove from the oven and let stand for 1 minute.
Loosen the cakes from around the edges of the pan;
using a palette knife. Turn the cakes out onto a clear
kitchen towel, remove the paper and invert them
onto a wire rack. When completely cool, sandwich
together with the jelly and cream, and sprinkle with
confectioners' sugar.

crumb cake

ingredients

serves 12

2 cups fresh blueberries
3 cup self-rising flour, plus extra
    for dusting
1¼ teaspoons salt
½ teaspoon apple pie spice
1¼ cups butter, at room
    temperature, plus extra for
    greasing
1¾ cups superfine sugar
½ teaspoon vanilla extract
½ teaspoon almond extract
2 extra-large eggs
1¼–1½ cups sour cream

crumb topping

½ cup butter, diced
1 cup all-purpose flour
2 tablespoons light brown sugar
1 tablespoon granulated sugar
heaping ¼ cup chopped blanched
    almonds

method

1 To make the crumb topping, rub the butter into the
  flour until the mixture resembles coarse breadcrumbs.
  Stir in both types of sugar and the almonds, then chill
  in the refrigerator.

2 Preheat the oven to 350°F. Grease a 13 x 9-inch
  rectangular cake pan and dust with flour. Dust the
  blueberries with 1 tablespoon of the flour and set
  aside. Sift the remaining flour into a bowl with the salt
  and apple pie spice and set aside.

3 Place the butter in a large bowl and, using an electric
  mixer, beat until soft and creamy. Add the sugar, vanilla
  extract, and almond extract, and continue beating until
  the batter is light and fluffy. Beat in the eggs one at a
  time, then beat in 1¼ cups of the sour cream. Beat in
  the flour until the batter is soft and falls easily from a
  spoon. Add the remaining sour cream, 1 tablespoon at
  a time, if necessary.

4 Add the blueberries and any loose flour to the batter
  and quickly fold in. Pour the batter into the prepared
  pan and smooth the surface. Pinch the topping into
  large crumbs and scatter evenly over the batter.

5 Bake in the preheated oven for 45–55 minutes until
  it comes away from the side of the pan. Transfer the
  pan to a wire rack and let cool completely. Cut into
  slices and serve straight from the pan.

lemon pound cake

ingredients

serves 8

butter, for greasing
1¾ cups all-purpose flour
2 teaspoons baking powder
1 cup superfine sugar
4 eggs
⅔ cup sour cream
grated rind of 1 large lemon
4 tablespoons lemon juice
⅔ cup sunflower oil

syrup

4 tablespoons confectioners' sugar
3 tablespoons lemon juice

method

1 Preheat the oven to 350°F. Lightly grease an 8-inch loose-bottom round cake pan and line the bottom with parchment paper.

2 Sift the flour and baking powder together into a mixing bowl and stir in the sugar.

3 In a separate bowl, whisk the eggs, sour cream, lemon rind, lemon juice, and oil together.

4 Pour the egg mixture into the dry ingredients and mix well until evenly combined.

5 Pour the batter into the prepared pan and bake in the preheated oven for 45–60 minutes, until risen and golden brown.

6 Meanwhile, to make the syrup, mix the confectioners' sugar and lemon juice together in a small saucepan. Stir over a low heat until just beginning to bubble and turn syrupy.

7 As soon as the cake comes out of the oven, pierce the surface with a fine toothpick, then brush the syrup over the top. Leave the cake to cool completely in the pan before turning it out and serving.

angel food cake

ingredients

serves 10

sunflower oil, for greasing
8 extra-large egg whites
1 teaspoon cream of tartar
1 teaspoon almond extract
1¼ cups superfine sugar
1 cup all-purpose flour, plus extra
     for dusting

to serve

2¼ cups summer berries
1 tablespoon lemon juice
2 tablespoons confectioners' sugar

method

1 Preheat the oven to 325°F. Brush the inside of a 7½-cup bundt or ring pan with oil and dust lightly with flour.

2 Whisk the egg whites in a clean, grease-free bowl until they hold soft peaks. Add the cream of tartar and whisk again until the whites are stiff but not dry.

3 Whisk in the almond extract, then add the sugar, a tablespoon at a time, whisking hard between each addition. Sift in the flour and fold in lightly and evenly, using a large metal spoon.

4 Spoon the batter into the prepared cake pan and tap on the counter to remove any large air bubbles. Bake in the preheated oven for 40–45 minutes, or until golden brown and firm to the touch.

5 Run the tip of a small knife around the edges of the cake to loosen it from the pan. Let cool in the pan for 10 minutes, then turn out onto a wire rack to finish cooling.

6 To serve, place the berries, lemon juice, and confectioners' sugar in a saucepan and heat gently until the sugar has dissolved. Serve with the cake.

devil's food cake

ingredients

serves 8–10

5 ounces semisweet chocolate,
    broken into pieces
scant ½ cup milk
2 tablespoons unsweetened cocoa
    powder
⅔ cup unsalted butter, plus extra
    for greasing
⅔ cup light brown sugar
3 eggs, separated
4 tablespoons sour cream
1¾ cups all-purpose flour
1 teaspoon baking soda

frosting

5 ounces semisweet chocolate,
    broken into pieces
⅓ cup unsweetened cocoa powder
4 tablespoons sour cream
1 tablespoon light corn syrup
3 tablespoons unsalted butter
4 tablespoons water
1¾ cups confectioners' sugar

method

1 Preheat the oven to 325°F. Grease two 8-inch cake pans
   and line the bottoms with nonstick parchment paper.

2 Place the chocolate, milk, and cocoa powder in a bowl
   over a saucepan of simmering water and heat gently,
   stirring, until melted. Remove from the heat.

3 In a large bowl beat the butter and brown sugar
   together until pale and fluffy. Beat in the egg yolks, the
   sour cream, and the melted chocolate mixture. Sift in
   the flour and baking soda, then fold in evenly. In a
   separate bowl, whisk the egg whites until stiff, then
   fold into the batter lightly and evenly.

4 Divide the batter between the cake pans,
   smooth level, and bake in the preheated oven for
   35–40 minutes, or until risen and firm to the touch.
   Cool in the pans for 10 minutes, then turn out onto a
   wire rack.

5 To make the frosting, put all the ingredients, except for
   the confectioners' sugar, into a saucepan and heat
   gently, until melted. Remove from the heat and sift in
   the sugar, stirring until smooth. Cool, stirring
   occasionally, until the mixture begins to thicken and
   hold its shape.

6 Split the cakes in half horizontally to make four layers.
   Sandwich them together with about a third of the
   frosting. Spread the remainder over the top and sides

oat & potato bread

ingredients

makes 1 loaf

vegetable oil, for greasing
2 mealy potatoes (about ½ pound)
3½ cups white bread flour,
    plus extra for dusting
1½ teaspoons salt
3 tablespoons butter, diced
1½ teaspoons active dry yeast
1½ tablespoons dark brown sugar
3 tablespoons rolled oats
2 tablespoons skim milk powder
scant 1 cup lukewarm water

topping

1 tablespoon water
1 tablespoon rolled oats

method

1 Grease a 2-pound loaf pan. Put the potatoes in a large saucepan, add water to cover, and bring to a boil. Cook for 20–25 minutes, until tender. Drain, then mash until smooth. Leave to cool.

2 Sift the flour and salt together into a warmed bowl. Rub in the butter with your fingertips. Stir in the yeast, sugar, oats, and milk powder. Mix in the mashed potato, then add the water and mix to a soft dough.

3 Place the dough onto a lightly floured work surface and knead for 5–10 minutes, or until smooth and elastic. Brush a bowl with oil and put the dough into it, cover with plastic wrap and let rise in a warm place for 1 hour, or until doubled in size.

4 Remove the dough again and knead lightly. Shape into a loaf and transfer to the prepared pan. Cover and leave to rise in a warm place for 30 minutes. Meanwhile, preheat the oven to 425°F.

5 To make the topping, brush the surface of the loaf with the water and carefully sprinkle over the oats. Bake in the preheated oven for 25–30 minutes, or until it sounds hollow when tapped on the bottom. Transfer to a wire rack and leave to cool slightly. Serve warm.

cornbread

ingredients

makes 1 small loaf

vegetable oil, for greasing
1½ cups all-purpose flour
1 teaspoon salt
4 teaspoons baking powder
1 teaspoon superfine sugar
2½ cups yellow cornmeal
¾ cup butter, softened
4 eggs
1 cup milk
3 tablespoons heavy cream

method

1 Preheat the oven to 400°F. Brush an 8-inch square cake pan with oil.

2 Sift the flour, salt, and baking powder together into a bowl. Add the sugar and cornmeal and stir to mix. Add the butter, cutting into the dry ingredients with a knife, then rub it in with your fingertips until the mixture resembles fine breadcrumbs.

3 Lightly beat the eggs in a bowl with the milk and cream, then stir into the cornmeal mixture until thoroughly combined.

4 Spoon the batter into the prepared pan and smooth the surface. Bake in the preheated oven for 30–35 minutes, until a toothpick inserted into the center of the loaf comes out clean. Remove the pan from the oven and let cool for 5–10 minutes, then cut into squares and serve warm.

variation

To add extra flavor and color, seed and skin one large red bell pepper. Dice finely and fold into the mixture. Or add one red chile, seeded and finely chopped.

index